PERSIAN FOR BEGINNERS

FIRST 1000 WORDS

EFFIE DELAROSA

CONTENTS

CONTENTS

CONTENTS

TALK
SOHBAT KARDAN
6
صحبت کردن

بله
Balé
Yes

خیر
Kheir
No

سلام
Salām
Hello

ممنون
Mamnoun
Thank You

خداحافظ
Khodāhāfez
Goodbye

لطفاً
Lotfan
Please

و
Va
And

یا
Yā
Or

این
In
This

من
Man
I

تو
To
You

او
Ou
He

او
Ou
She

ما
Mā
We

آنها
Ānhā
They

صحبت کردن

7 SOHBAT KARDAN

TALK

متاسفم
Moteasefam
Sorry
اما
Ammā
But
عصر بخیر
Asr Bekheir
Good evening
زیرا
Zirā
Because
بفرمایید
Befarmāeed
Welcome
کجا
Kojā
Where
چه
Ché
What
چقدر
Cheghadr
1
2
How much
کدام
Kodām
Which
عالی
Āali
Awesome
بامزه
Bāmazzé
Cute
کمک
Komak
Help
اگر
Agar
If
چه‌وقت
Chevaght
When
چرا
Cherā
Why

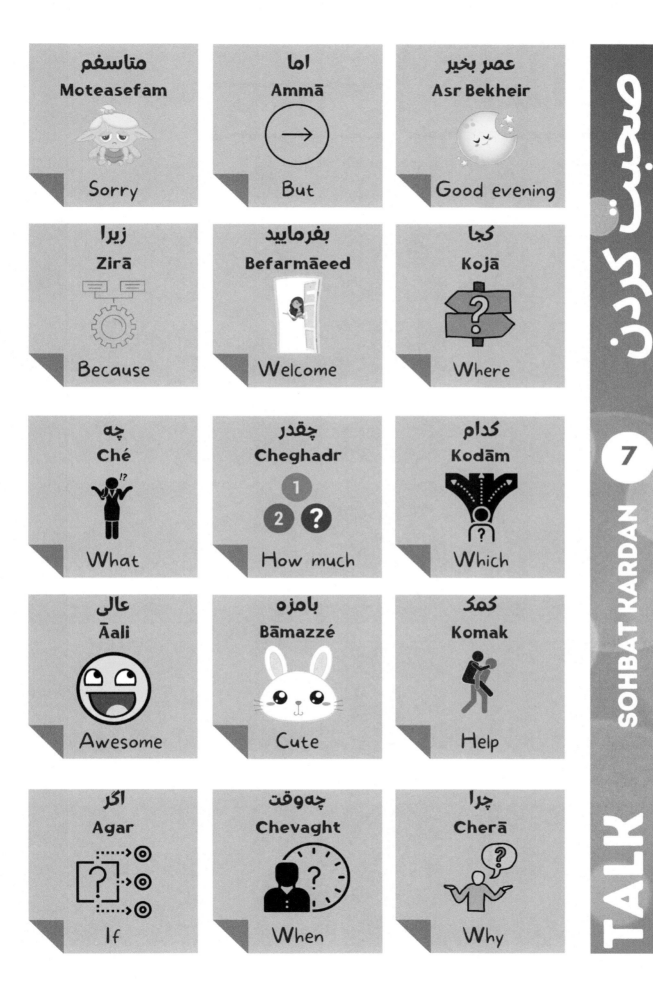

اعداد

adād

numbers

0 صفر Sefr Zero	1 یک Yek One	2 دو Do Two
3 سه Sé Three	4 چهار Chahār Four	5 پنج Panj Five
6 شش Shesh Six	7 هفت Haft Seven	8 هشت Hasht Eight
9 نه Noh Nine	10 ده Dah Ten	15 پانزده Pānzdah Fifteen
20 بیست Bist Twenty	100 صد Sad One Hundred	1000 هزار Hezār One Thousand

مادر
Mādar
Mother

پدر
Pedar
Father

برادر
Barādar
Brother

خواهر
Khāhar
Sister

مادربزرگ
Mādarbozorg
Grandmother

پدربزرگ
Pedarbozorg
Grandfather

پسر
Pesar
Son

دختر
Dokhtar
Daughter

عمه/خاله
Amme/Khāle
Aunt

عمو/دایی
Amou/Dayi
Uncle

نوه دختر
Navé Dokhtar
Granddaughter

نوه پسر
Navé Pesar
Grandson

زن
Zan
Wife

شوهر
Shohar
Husband

صبحانه
Sobhāné
Breakfast

ناهار
Nāhār
Lunch

شام
Shām
Dinner

وعده غذایی
Vadé Ghazāyi
Meal

نان
Nān
Bread

پنیر
Panir
Cheese

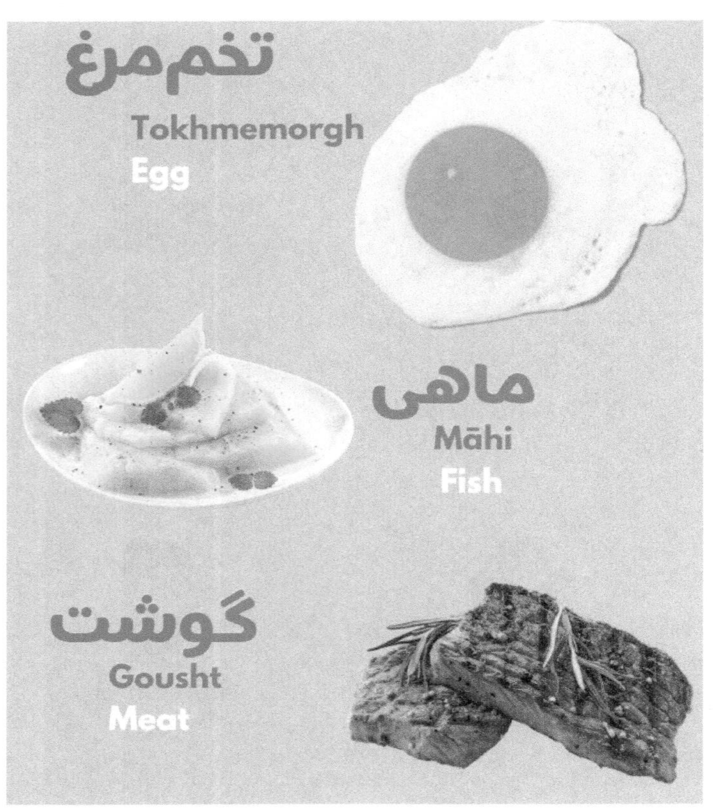

تخم‌مرغ
Tokhmemorgh
Egg

ماهی
Māhi
Fish

گوشت
Gousht
Meat

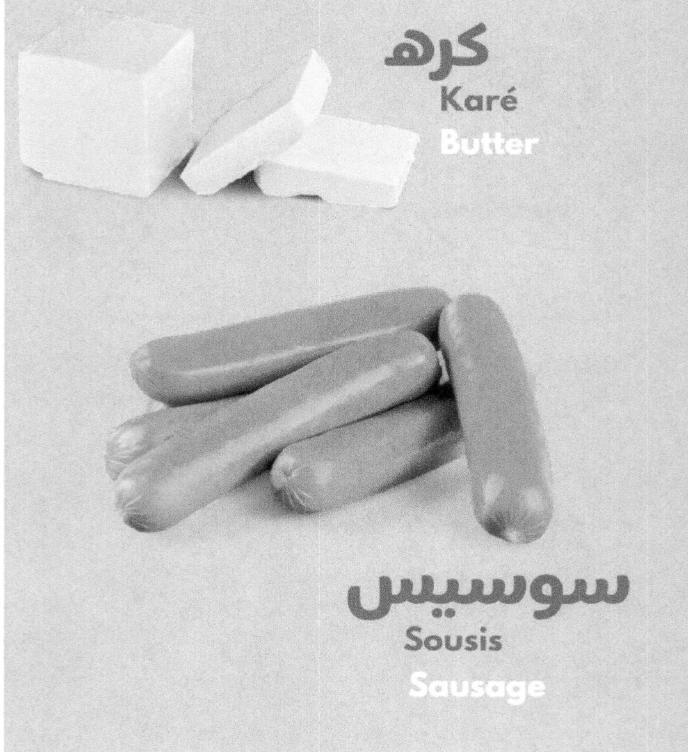

کره
Karé
Butter

سوسیس
Sousis
Sausage

ماست
Māst
Yogurt

کیک
Keik
Cake

شکلات
Shokolāt
Chocolate

نمک
Namak
Salt

شکر
Shekar
Sugar

فلفل
Felfel
Pepper

نوشیدنی
Noushidani
Drink

آرد
Ārd
Flour

آبنبات
Ābnabāt
Lollipop

عسل
Asal
Honey

دونات
Donāt
Doughnut

بستنی
Bastani
Ice Cream

آب
Āb
Water

قهوه
Ghahvé
Coffee

شیر
Shīr
Milk

آب پرتقال
Āb Porteghāl
Orange Juice

چای
Chāy
Tea

شکلات داغ
Shokolaté Dāgh
Hot Chocolate

غذا
Ghazā
Food

دسر
Deser
Dessert

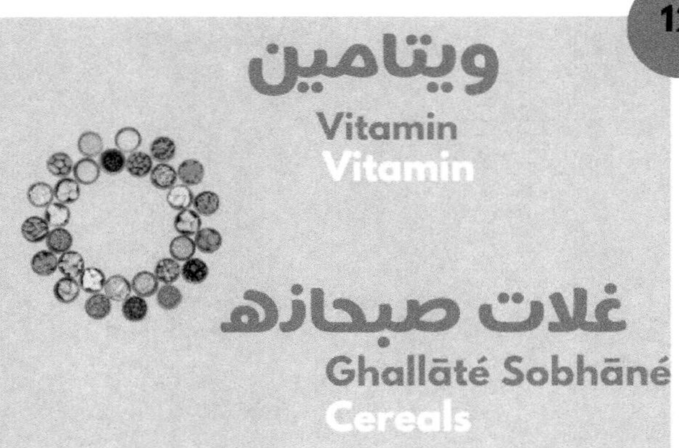

ویتامین
Vitamin
Vitamin

غلات صبحانه
Ghallāté Sobhāné
Cereals

پیاز
Piyāz
Onion

لوبیا
Loubyā
Beans

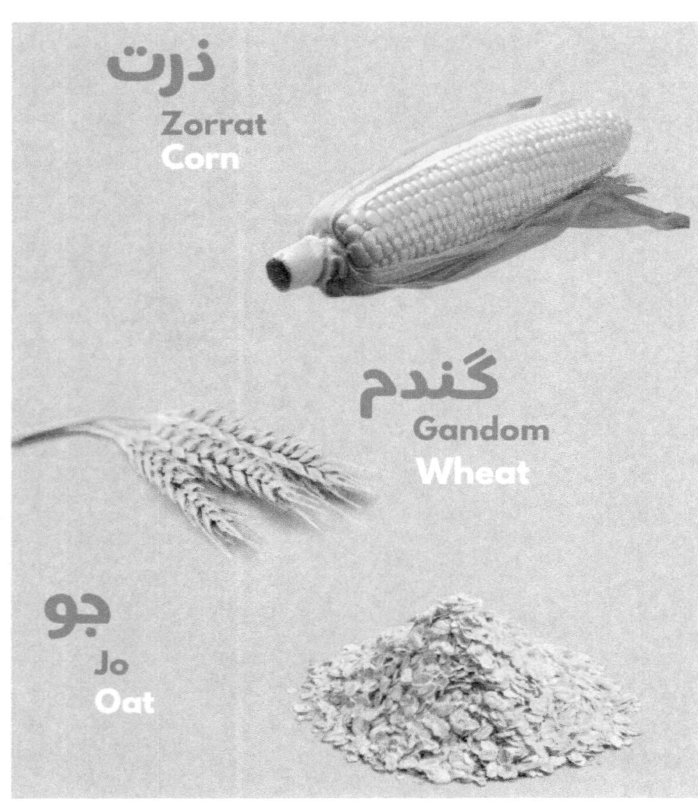

ذرت
Zorrat
Corn

گندم
Gandom
Wheat

جو
Jo
Oat

سس کچاپ
Sosé Kachāp
Ketchup

خردل
Khardal
Mustard

ادویه‌جات
Adviyejāt
Spices

روغن
Roghan
Oil

برنج
Berenj
Rice

پاستا
Pāstā
Pasta

وسایل نقلیه
vasāyelé naghliyé

vehicles

هواپیما
HAVĀPEYMA
AIRPLANE

قایق
GHĀYEGH
BOAT

کشتی
KASHTI
SHIP

ماشین
MĀSHIN
CAR

موتور سیکلت
MOTORSIKLET
MOTORBIKE

قطار
GHATĀR
TRAIN

تراکتور
TERĀKTOR
TRACTOR

دوچرخه
DOCHARKHÉ
BICYCLE

اتوبوس
OTOBOUS
BUS

تاکسی
TĀKSI
TAXI

مترو
METRO
SUBWAY

کامیون
KĀMIYON
TRUCK

آمبولانس
ĀMBOLANS
AMBULANCE

هلیکوپتر
HELIKOPTER
HELICOPTER

قطار برقی
GHATĀRÉ BARGHI
TRAM

مسافرت

mosāferat — **travel**

تعطیلات
TATILĀT
HOLIDAY

فرودگاه
FOROUDGĀH
AIRPORT

ایستگاه قطار
ISTGĀHÉ GHATĀR
TRAIN STATION

بندر
BANDAR
PORT

توریست
TOURIST
TOURIST

هتل
HOTEL
HOTEL

خانه
KHĀNÉ
HOUSE

آپارتمان
ĀPĀRTEMĀN
APARTMENT

چمدان
CHAMEDĀN
SUITCASE

پاسپورت
PĀSPORT
PASSPORT

نقشه
NAGHSHÉ
MAP

استخر شنا
ESTAKHRÉ SHENĀ

SWIMMING POOL

جاده
JĀDDÉ
ROAD

خیابان
KHIYĀBĀN
STREET

پیاده‌روی
PIYĀDÉ RAVI
WALK

حیوانات

HEYVĀNĀT

ANIMALS

پرنده
Parandé

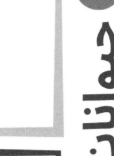

Bird

گربه
Gorbé

Cat

سگ
Sag

Dog

اردک
Ordak

Duck

موش
Moush

Mouse

کبوتر
Kaboutar

Pigeon

خرگوش
Khargoush

Rabbit

فیل
Fil

Elephant

میمون
Meymoun

Monkey

مرغ
Morgh

Chicken

گاو
Gāv

Cow

خر
Khar

Donkey

بز
Boz

Goat

اسب
Asb

Horse

خوک
Khouk

Pig

حیوانات
HEYVĀNĀT
ANIMALS

گوسفند
Gousfand
Sheep

غاز
Ghāz
Goose

خرس
Khers
Bear

شتر
Shotor
Camel

قورباغه
Ghourbāghé
Frog

مار
Mār
Snake

لاکپشت
Lākposht
Turtle

گرگ
Gorg
Wolf

تمساح
Temsāh
Crocodile

دایناسور
Dāynāsor
Dinosaur

زرافه
Zarrāfé
Giraffe

کانگورو
Kāngoro
Kangaroo

مارمولک
Mārmoulak
Lizard

ببر
Babr
Tiger

گوره‌خر
Goré Khar
Zebra

کوسه
Kousé
Shark

خرچنگ
Kharchang
Crab

دلفین
Dolfin

Dolphin

عروس دریایی
Arousé Daryāyi

Jellyfish

لابستر
Lābester

Lobster

اسب دریایی
Asbé Daryāyi

Seahorse

سفره‌ماهی
Sofré Māhi

Ray

اختاپوس
Okhtāpous

Octopus

پروانه
Parvāné

Butterfly

سوسک
Sousk

Cockroach

عنکبوت
Ankabout

Spider

خزوک
Khazouk

Beetle

سنجاقک
Sanjāghak

Dragonfly

مورچه
Mourché

Ant

زنبور
Zanbour

Bee

روز
ROUZ

DAY

دوشنبه
DOSHANBÉ
MONDAY

سه شنبه
SESHANBÉ
TUESDAY

چهارشنبه
CHAHĀRSHANBÉ
WEDNESDAY

پنج شنبه
PANJSHANBÉ
THURSDAY

جمعه
JOMÉ
FRIDAY

شنبه
SHANBÉ
SATURDAY

یک شنبه
YEKSHANBÉ
SUNDAY

هفته
HAFTÉ
WEEK

زمان
ZAMĀN

TIME

ساعت
SĀAT
HOUR

دقیقه
DAGHIGHÉ
MINUTE

سال
SĀL

YEAR

ماه
MĀH

MONTH

ژانویه
ZHĀNVIYÉ
JANUARY

فوریه
FEVRIYÉ
FEBRUARY

مارس
MĀRS
MARCH

آوریل
ĀVRIL
APRIL

مه
MEH
MAY

ژوئن
ZHOUAN
JUNE

ژوئیه
ZHOUIYÉ
JULY

اوت
OUT
AUGUST

سپتامبر
SEPTĀMBR
SEPTEMBER

اکتبر
OCTOBR
OCTOBER

نوامبر
NOVĀMBR
NOVEMBER

دسامبر
DESĀMBR
DECEMBER

فصل
Fasl
Season

بهار
Bahār
Spring

زمستان
Zemestān
Winter

تابستان
Tābestān
Summer

پاییز
Pāyiz
Autumn

باد
Bād
Wind

باران
Bārān
Rain

رعد و برق
Rad-o Bargh
Thunderstorm

صبح
Sobh
Morning

بعد از ظهر
Bad Az Zohr
Afternoon

شب
Shab
Night

آب و هوا
Āb-o Havā
Climate

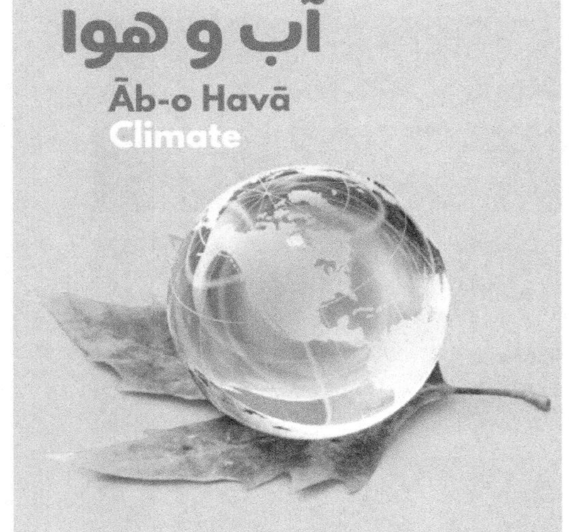

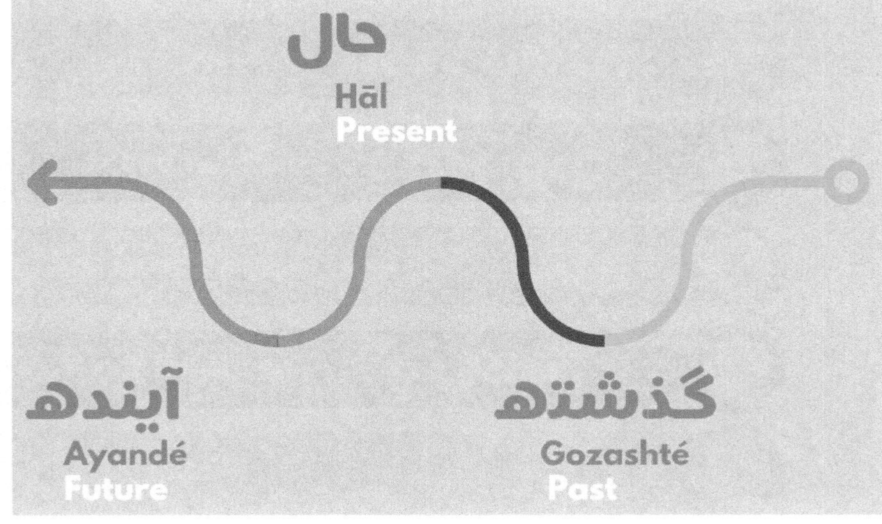

حال
Hāl
Present

گذشته
Gozashté
Past

آینده
Ayandé
Future

افعال
AFĀL

VERBS

داشتن	dāshtan	have
بودن	boudan	be
انجام دادن	anjām dādan	do
گفتن	goftan	say
توانستن	tavānestan	can
رفتن	raftan	go
دیدن	didan	see
دانستن	dānestan	know
خواستن	khāstan	want
آمدن	āmadan	come
احتیاج داشتن	ehtiyāj dāshtan	need
مجبور بودن	majbour bodan	have to
اعتقاد داشتن	eteghād dāshtan	believe
پیدا کردن	peydā kardan	find
دادن	dādan	give

افعال

AFĀL

VERBS

گرفتن	gereftan	take
صحبت کردن	sohbat kardan	talk
گذاشتن	gozāshtan	put
به نظر رسیدن	bé nazar residan	seem
ترک کردن	tark kardan	leave
ماندن	māndan	stay
فکر کردن	fekr kardan	think
به نظر رسیدن	bé nazar residan	look
جواب دادن	javāb dādan	answer
منتظر ماندن	montazer māndan	wait
زندگی کردن	zendegi kardan	live
متوجه شدن	motevajeh shodan	understand
وارد شدن	vāred shodan	come in
شدن	shodan	become
برگشتن	bargashtan	come back

افعال

AFĀL

VERBS

نوشتن	neveshtan	write
زنگ زدن	zang zadan	call
افتادن	oftādan	fall
شروع کردن	shorou kardan	start
دنبال کردن	donbāl kardan	follow
نشان دادن	neshān dādan	show
خندیدن	khandidan	laugh
لبخند زدن	labkhand zadan	smile
بھ یاد آوردن	be yād āvardan	remember
بازی کردن	bāzi kardan	play
خوردن	khordan	eat
خواندن	khāndan	read
گرفتن	gereftan	get
گریھ کردن	geryé kardan	cry
توضیح دادن	tozih dādan	explain

افعال

AFĀL

VERBS

آواز خواندن	āvāz khāndan	sing
لمس کردن	lams kardan	touch
بو کردن	bou kardan	smell
نفس کشیدن	nafas keshidan	breathe
شنیدن	shenidan	hear
رنگ کردن	rang kardan	paint
مطالعه کردن	motāleé kardan	study
جشن گرفتن	jashn gereftan	celebrate
انتخاب کردن	entekhāb kardan	choose
جست و جو کردن	jost-o jou kardan	search
پرسیدن	porsidan	ask
لذت بردن	lezzat bordan	enjoy
تصور کردن	tasavvor kardan	imagine
نوشیدن	noushidan	drink
تغییر دادن	taghyir dādan	change

الفبا
Alefbā
Alphabet

مداد
Medād
Pencil

دفترچه
Daftarché
Notebook

کیف مدرسه
Kif-é Madresé
Schoolbag

قیچی
Gheychi
Scissors

دانش‌آموز
Dānesh Amouz
Student

کلاس درس
Kelas-é Dars
Classroom

دوستان
Doustān
Friends

استاد
Ostād
Professor

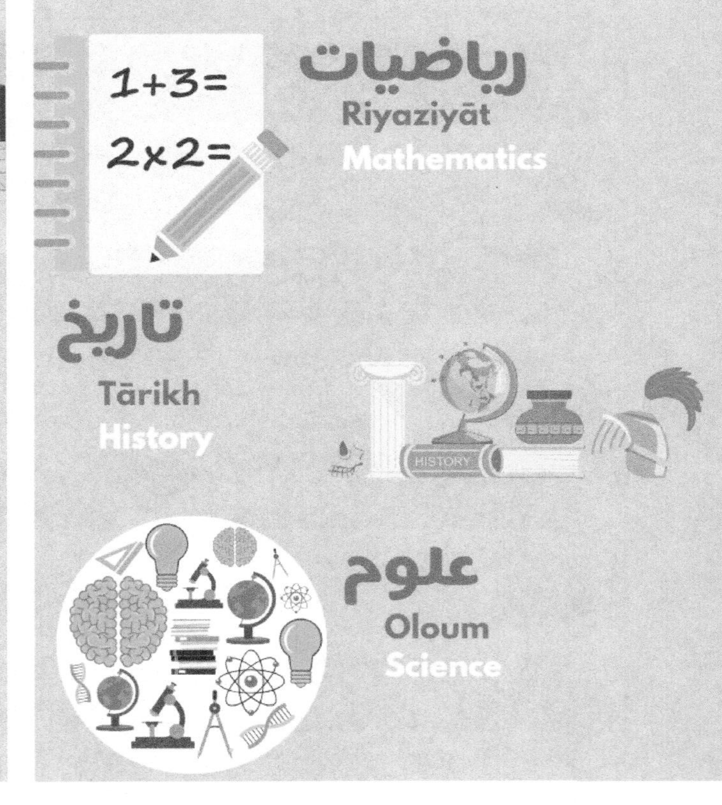

ریاضیات
Riyaziyāt
Mathematics

تاریخ
Tārikh
History

علوم
Oloum
Science

مدرسه
Madresé
School

هنر
Honar
Arts

جغرافیا
Joghrāfiā
Geography

shoghl — job

پرستار **PARASTĀR** **NURSE**	کشاورز **KESHĀVARZ** **FARMER**	معمار **MEMĀR** **ARCHITECT**

مهندس **MOHANDES** **ENGINEER**	کارگر **KĀRGAR** **LABORER**	آتش‌نشان **ĀTASH NESHĀN** **FIREFIGHTER**

باغبان **BĀGHBĀN** **GARDENER**	وکیل **VAKIL** **LAWYER**	خلبان **KHALABĀN** **PILOT**

بازیگر **BĀZIGAR** **ACTOR**	دندانپزشک **DANDĀNPEZESHK** **DENTIST**	مکانیک **MEKĀNIK** **MECHANIC**

رفتگر **ROFTEGAR** **DUSTMAN**	حسابدار **HESĀBDĀR** **ACCOUNTANT**	روانشناس **RAVĀNSHENĀS** **PSYCHOLOGIST**

شغل
shoghl
job

خبرنگار **KHABARNEGĀR** JOURNALIST	نجار **NAJJĀR** CARPENTER	نوازنده **NAVĀZANDÉ** MUSICIAN
لوله‌کش **LOLÉ KESH** PLUMBER	آشپز **ĀSHPAZ** COOK	نویسنده **NEVISANDÉ** WRITER
آرایشگر **ĀRĀYESHGAR** HAIRDRESSER	منشی **MONSHI** SECRETARY	راننده **RĀNANADÉ** DRIVER
پلیس **POLIS** POLICEMAN	دکتر **DOCTOR** DOCTOR	دامپزشک **DĀMPEZESHK** VETERINARIAN
عینک‌ساز **EYNAK SĀZ** OPTICIAN	 پزشک اطفال **PEZESHK-É ATFĀL** PEDIATRICIAN	پیشخدمت **PISHKHEDMAT** WAITER

آلو
Ālou
PLUM

هلو
Holou
PEACH

گیلاس
Gilas
CHERRY

سیب
Sīb
APPLE

انگور
Angour
GRAPE

هندوانه
Hendavāné
WATERMELON

آناناس
Ānānās
PINEAPPLE

توت فرنگی
Tout Farangi
STRAWBERRY

تمشک
Tameshk
RASPBERRY

گلابی
Golābi
PEAR

موز
Mouz
BANANA

طالبی
Tālebi
MELON

لیمو
Limou
LEMON

توت سیاه
Tout-é Siyāh
BLACKBERRY

پرتقال
Porteghāl
ORANGE

سبزیجات

SABZIJĀT

VEGETABLES

قارچ
Ghārch
MUSHROOM

بروکلی
Boroukli
BROCCOLI

کلم
Kalam
CABBAGE

مارچوبه
Mārchoubé
ASPARAGUS

خیار
Khiyār
CUCUMBER

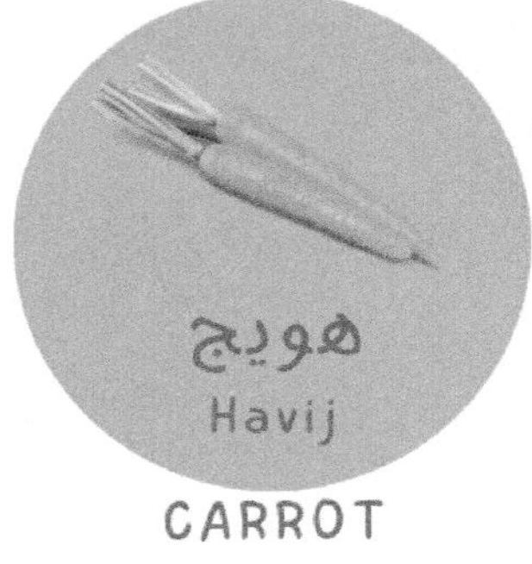
هویج
Havij
CARROT

تربچه
Torobché
RADISH

کاهو
Kāhou
LETTUCE

سیب زمینی
Sibzamini
POTATO

گوجه فرنگی
Gojé Farangi
TOMATO

آووکادو
Āvokado
AVOCADO

تره فرنگی
Taré Farangi
LEEK

چغندر
Ghoghobdar
BEETROOT

بادمجان
Bādemjān
EGGPLANT

کنگر فرنگی
Kangar Farangi
ARTICHOKE

احساسات

Ehsāsāt

Feelings

آرام
Ārām
Calm

خوشحال
Khosh Hāl
Happy

ناامید
Nāomid
Disappointed

هیجان‌زده
Hayajān Zadé
Excited

وحشت‌زده
Vahshat Zadé
Frightened

بدخلق
Bad Kholgh
Grumpy

عاشق
Āshegh
In Love

شگفت‌زده
Shegeft Zadé
Surprised

خجالت‌زده
Khejālat Zadé
Shy

مغرور
Maghrour
Proud

عصبانی
Asabāni
Angry

گیج
Gīj
Confused

خسته
Khasté
Tired

عصبی
Asabi
Nervous

کنجکاو
Konjkāv
Curious

صفت‌ها

sefathā

adjectives

خارق العاده	khārgholādé	fantastic
عجیب	ajib	weird
دشوار	doshvār	hard
خنده‌دار	khandedār	funny
عجیب	ajib	strange
آسان	āsān	easy
غیرممکن	gheyré momken	impossible
جوان	javān	young
درست	dorost	correct
آزاد	āzād	free
بیمار	bimār	sick
یکسان	yeksān	same
فقیر	faghir	poor
ممکن	momken	possible
تمیز	tamiz	clean

صفت‌ها

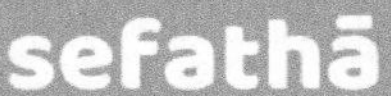

کثیف	kasif	dirty
ساده	sādé	simple
ناراحت	nārāhat	sad
خالی	khāli	empty
خوب	khoub	good
نرم	narm	soft
غلط	ghalat	false
بزرگ	bozorg	big
بد	bad	bad
جدی	jeddi	serious
پیر	pīr	old
درست	dorost	true
زیبا	zibā	beautiful
گرم	garm	hot
سرد	sard	cold

صفت ها

sefathā

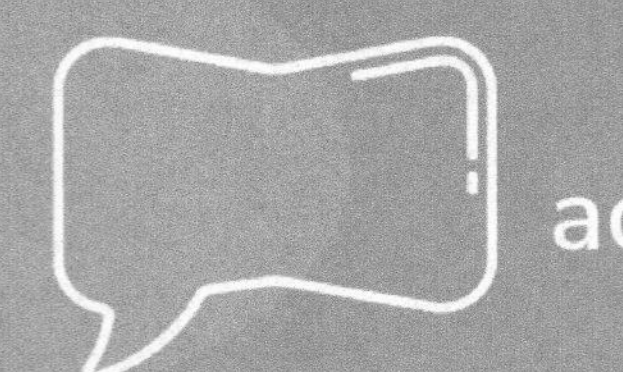

adjectives

گران	gerān	expensive
روشن	roshan	clear
آخرین	ākharin	last
متفاوت	motefāvet	different
قوی	ghavi	strong
خوب	khoub	nice
زیاد	ziyād	high
انسان	ensān	human
مهم	mohem	important
زیبا	zibā	pretty
سبک	sabok	light
کوچک	kouchak	small
جدید	jadid	new
پر	por	full
اول	aval	first

علف
Alaf
Grass
حشره
Hasharé
Insect
گل
Gol
Flower
هوا
Havā
Air
برف
Barf
Snow
کوه
Kouh
Mountain

ابر
Abr
Cloud
آسمان
Āsemān
Sky
مه
Meh
Fog

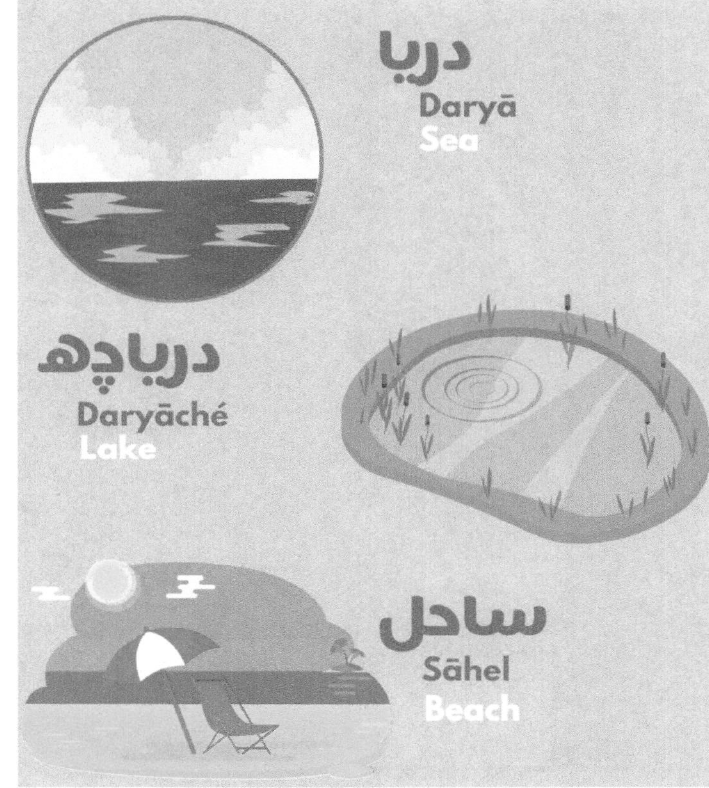
دریا
Daryā
Sea
دریاچه
Daryāché
Lake
ساحل
Sāhel
Beach

خورشید
Khorshid
Sun

جنگل
Jangal
Forest
درخت
Derakht
Tree

CULTURE

FARHANG

فرهنگ

روزنامه
Rouznāmé
NEWSPAPER

سینما
Sinemā
CINEMA

تلویزیون
Televizyon
TELEVISION

کتاب
Ketāb
BOOK

مجسمه
Mojasamé
SCULPTURE

عکاسی
Akāsi
PHOTOGRAPHY

موسیقی
Mousighi
MUSIC

کنسرت
Konsert
CONCERT

فیلم
Film
MOVIE

رایانه
Rāyāné
COMPUTER

فرهنگ لغت
Farhang-é loghat
DICTIONARY

نقاشی
Naghāshi
PAINTING

موزه
Mozé
MUSEUM

اپرا
Operā
OPERA

تئاتر
Teātr
THEATER

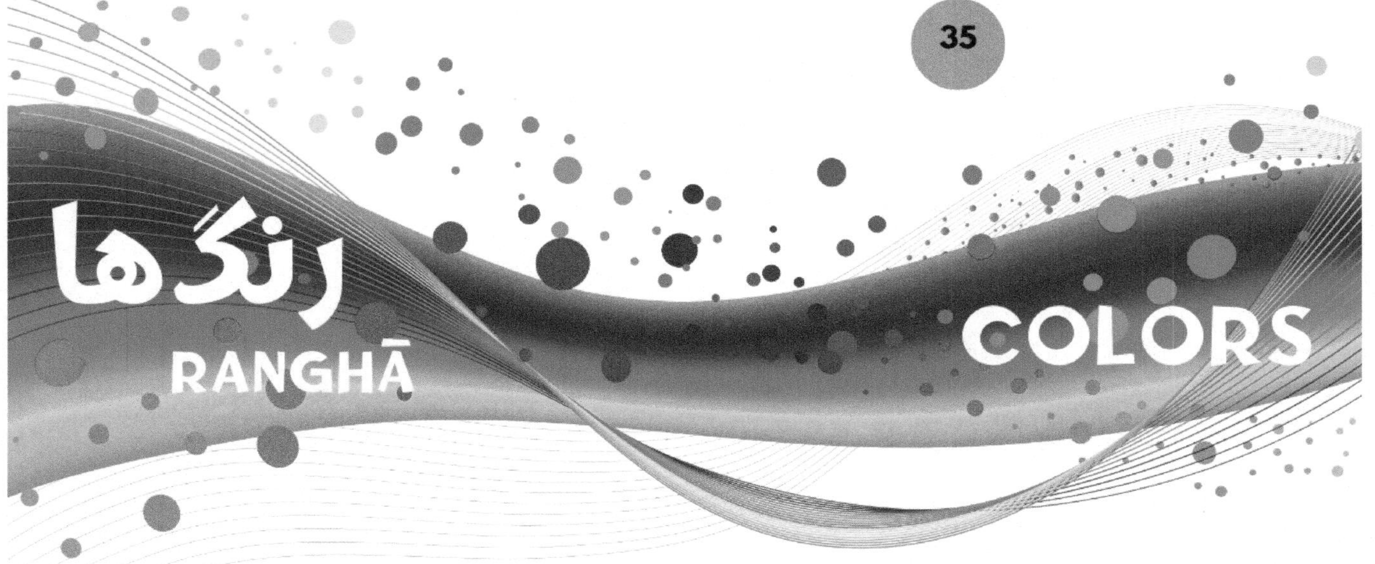

آبی ābi	blue
بنفش banafsh	purple
صورتی sourati	pink
قرمز ghermez	red
نارنجی nāranji	orange
زرد zard	yellow
سبز sabz	green
سیاه siyāh	black
سفید sefid	white
قهوه‌ای ghahvei	brown
طلایی talāyi	gold
خاکستری khākestari	gray
نقره‌ای noghrei	silver
رنگین کمان rangin kamān	rainbow

در جلوی	dar jeloyé	in front of
پشت	posht	behind
چپ	chap	left
راست	rāst	right
مرکز	markaz	middle
مربع	moraba	square
دایره	dāyeré	circle
مستطیل	mostatil	rectangle
مکعب	mokaab	cube
لوزی	louzi	diamond
خط	khat	line
غرب	gharb	west
شرق	shargh	east
شمال	shomāl	north
جنوب	jonoub	south

خانه
KHANÉ
HOME

آشپزخانه ĀSHPAZ KHĀNÉ	در DAR	اتاق ناهارخوری OTĀGHÉ NĀHĀRKHORI	حمام HAMMĀM
KITCHEN	DOOR	DINING ROOM	BATHROOM

پنجره PANJARÉ	پله PELLÉ	زیر شیروانی ZIR SHIRVĀNI	هال HĀL
WINDOW	STAIRS	ATTIC	HALL

اداره EDĀRÉ	بالکن BALKON	زیرزمین ZIRZAMIN	همسایه HAMSĀYÉ
OFFICE	BALCONY	BASEMENT	NEIGHBOR

باغچه BĀGHCHÉ	اتاق خواب OTĀGH KHĀB
GARDEN	BEDROOM

خانه
KHĀNÉ
HOME

فر
FER
OVEN

شوفاژ
SHOUFAZH
RADIATOR

مبل
MOBL
SOFA

یخچال
YAKHCHĀL
FRIDGE

آباژور
ĀBĀZHOR
LAMP

سینک ظرفشویی
SINK-É ZARFSHOUYI
SINK

تلفن
TELEFON
TELEPHONE

لیوان
LIVĀN
GLASS

بشقاب
BOSHGHĀB
PLATE

آینه
ĀYNÉ
MIRROR

ساعت
SĀAT
CLOCK

صندلی
SANDALI
CHAIR

تختخواب
TAKHT-É KHĀB
BED

میز
MĪZ
TABLE

خانه
KHĀNÉ

HOME

دیوار DIVĀR	پشت بام POSHT-É BĀM	فریزر FERIZER	کمد دیواری KOMOD DIVĀRI
WALL 	ROOF 	FREEZER 	CUPBOARD 
گیاه GIYĀH	شومینه SHOUMINÉ	جارو برقی JĀROU BARGHI	شیر آب SHIR-É ĀB
PLANT 	FIREPLACE 	VACUUM CLEANER 	TAP 
ظرفشویی ZARFSHOUYI	مایکروویو MAYKROVEIV	فرش FARSH	زنگ در ZANG-Ê DAR
DISHWASHER 	MICROWAVE 	CARPET 	DOORBELL 

شاتر پنجره SHATERÉ PANJARE	کلید KELID
SHUTTER 	KEY 

خانه

KHĀNÉ

HOME

حوله
HOLÉ
TOWEL

ملحفه
MALHAFÉ
BED SHEET

صابون
SĀBOUN
SOAP

شانه
SHĀNÉ
COMB

پرده
PARDÉ
CURTAIN

فنجان
FENJĀN
CUP

دوش
DOUSH
SHOWER

لامپ
LĀMP
LIGHTBULB

چنگال
CHANGĀL
FORK

قاشق
GHĀSHOGH
SPOON

چاقو
CHĀGHOU
KNIFE

وان حمام
VĀ-É HAMMĀM
BATHTUB

بطری
BOTRI
BOTTLE

سطل زباله
SATLÉ ZOBĀLÉ
GARBAGE CAN

حروف اضافه
horoufé ezāfé

prepositions

برای	barāyé	for
بعد از	bad az	after
قبل از	ghabl az	before
با	bā	with
دربارہ	darbāreyé	about
بہ	bé	against
در	dar	in
بدون	bedouné	without
از	az	since
سراسر	sarāsar	around
روی	rouyé	on
مانند	manandé	like
در طول	dar toulé	during
بین	beyné	between
اهل	ahlé	from

بدن **badan** **body** 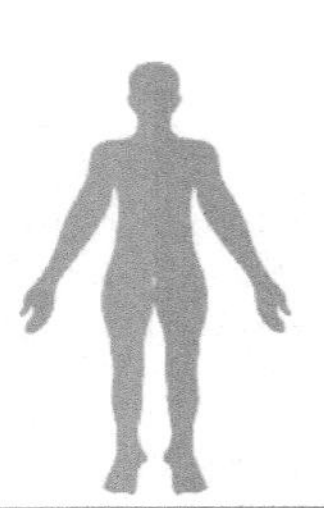	**سر** **sar** **head** 	**دست** **dast** **hand** 
مو **mou** **hair** 	**صورت** **sourat** **face** 	**انگشت** **angosht** **finger** 
گوش **goush** **ear** 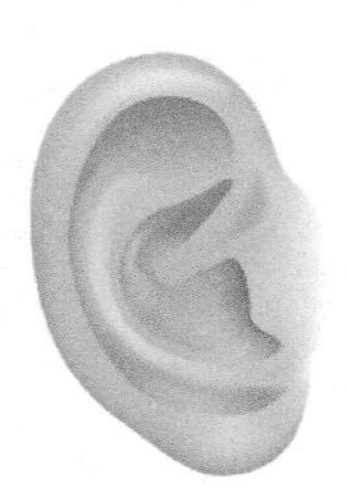	**چشم** **chashm** **eyes** 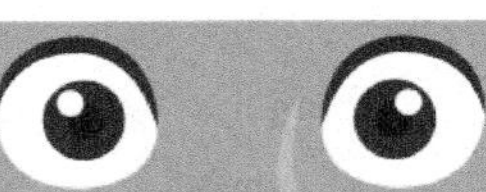	**ناخن** **nākhon** **nail** 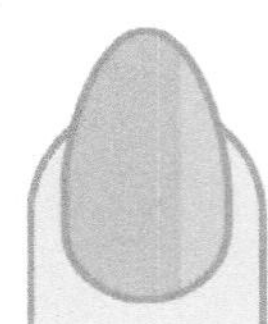
بینی **bini** **nose** 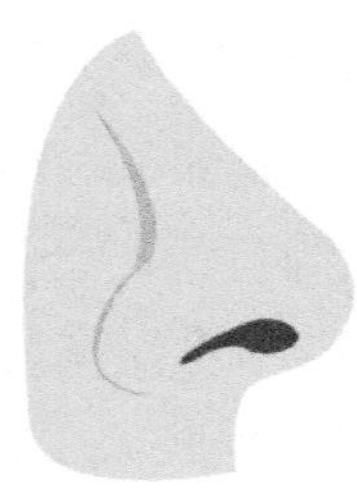	**دهان** **dahan** **mouth** 	**پا** **pā** **leg** 
دندان **dandān** **tooth** 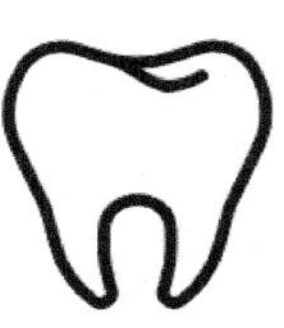	**لب** **lab** **lips** 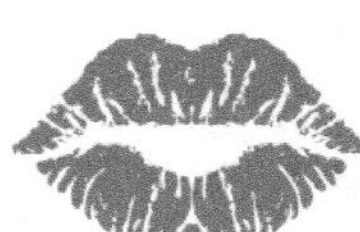	**پا** **pā** **foot** 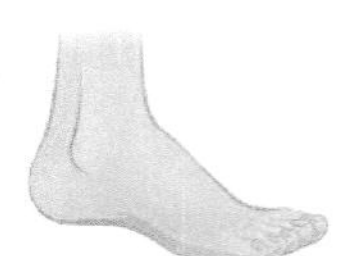

مغز
maghz
brain

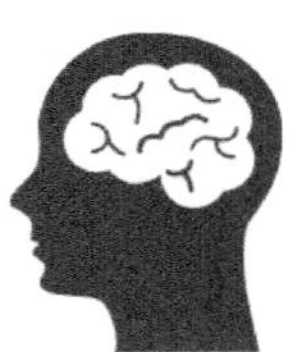

خون
khoun
blood

قلب
ghalb
heart

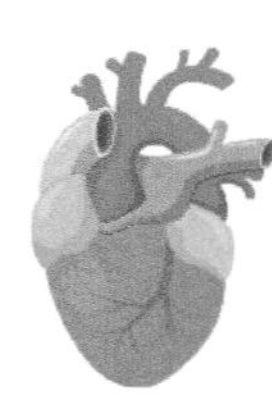

معده
medé
stomach

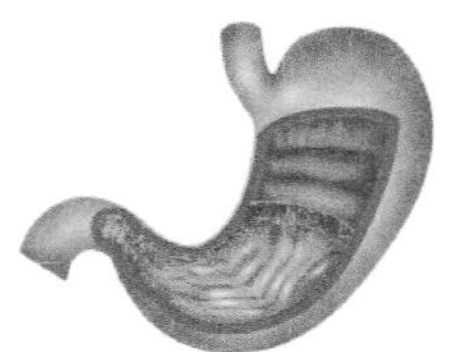

کبد
kabéd
liver

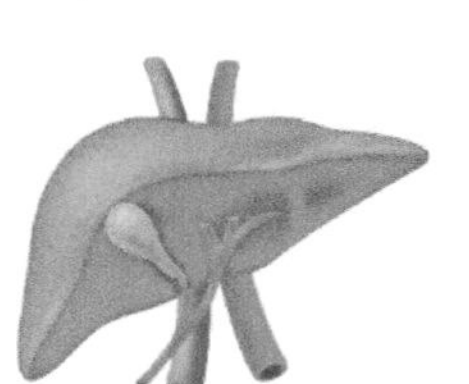

کلیه
koliyé
kidney

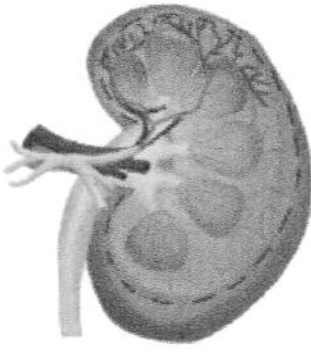

شش
shosh
lungs

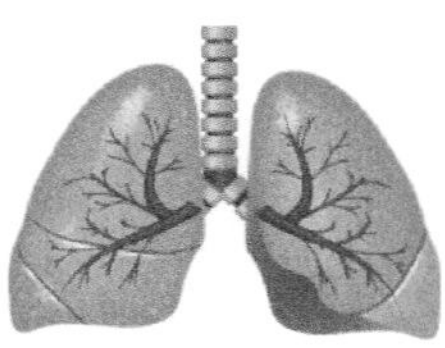

روده
roudé
intestine

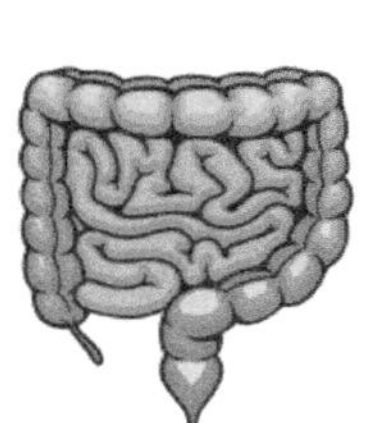

ناف
nāf
navel

کتف
ketf
shoulder

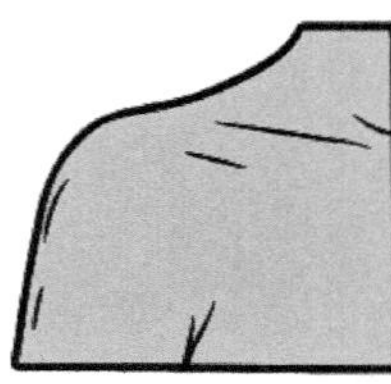

زبان
zabān
tongue

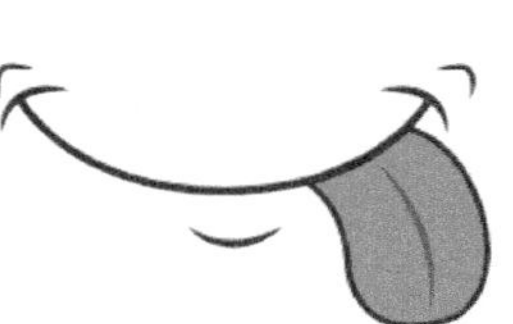

شکم
skekam
belly

لگن
lagan
hip

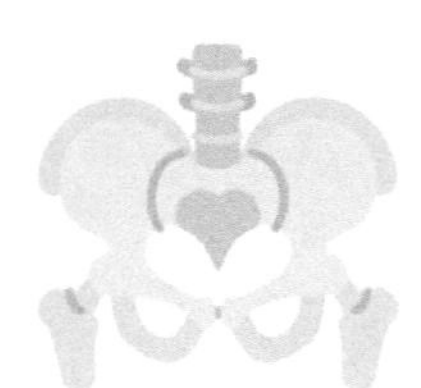

زانو
zānou
knee

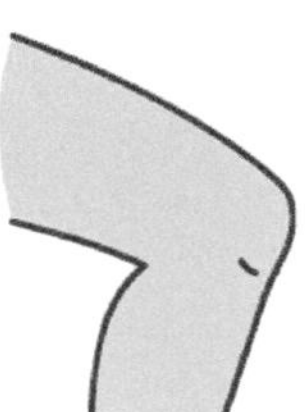

قوزک پا
ghouzak-é pā
Ankle

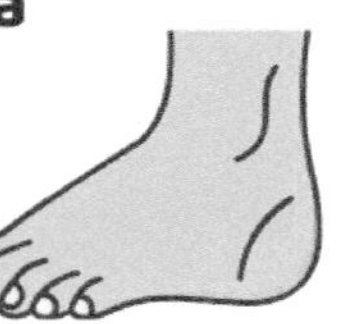

پوست
poust
skin

استخوان
ostokhān
bone

جمجمه
jomjomé
skull

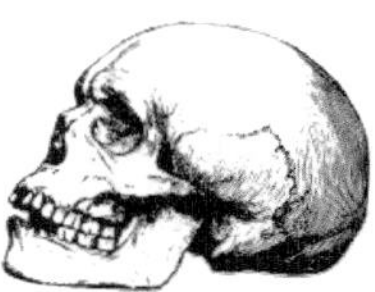

گردن
gardan
neck

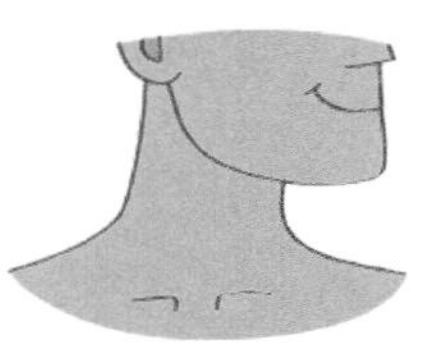

مچ دست
moch-é Dast
wrist

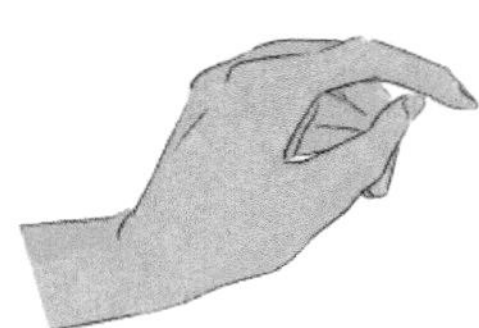

ابرو
abrou
eyebrow

گلو
galou
throat

پلک
pelk
eyelid

چانه
chané
chin

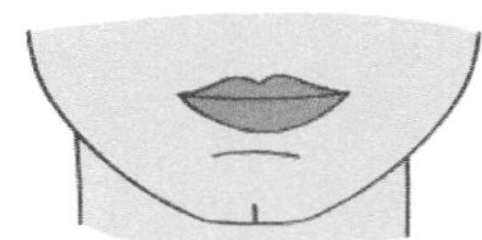

ریش
rish
beard

سبیل
sebil
mustache

ماهیچه
mahiché
muscle

آرنج
aranj
elbow

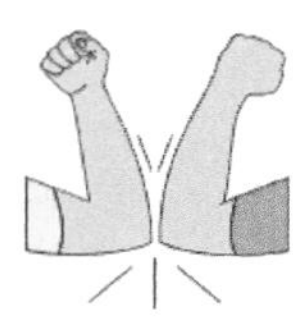

انگشت پا
angosht-é pā
toe

گونه
gouné
cheek

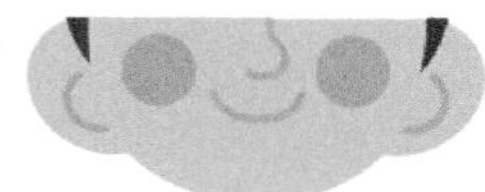

زمان
zamān

time

دیروز	dirouz	yesterday
امروز	emrouz	today
فردا	fardā	tomorrow
الان	alān	now
زود	zoud	soon
دیر	dir	late
اینجا	injā	here
فاصله	faselé	distance
طلوع خورشید	toloué khorshid	sunrise
ظهر	zohr	noon
عصر	asr	evening
نیمه‌شب	nimé shab	midnight
دهه	dahé	decade
قرن	gharn	century
هزاره	hezāré	millennium

کشور KESHVAR COUNTRY

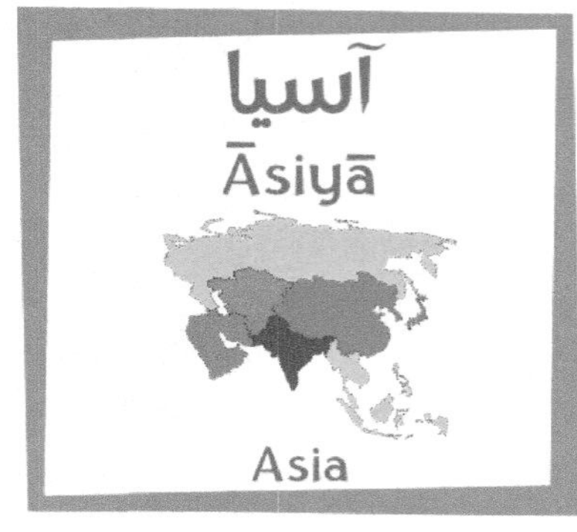
آسیا
Āsiyā
Asia

آفریقا
Āfrighā
Africa

اروپا
Oroupā
Europe

آلمان
Ālmān
Germany

انگلیس
Engelis
England

آمریکا
Āmricā
America

ایتالیا
Itāliyā
Italy

اسپانیا
Espāniyā
Spain

فرانسه
Farānsé
France

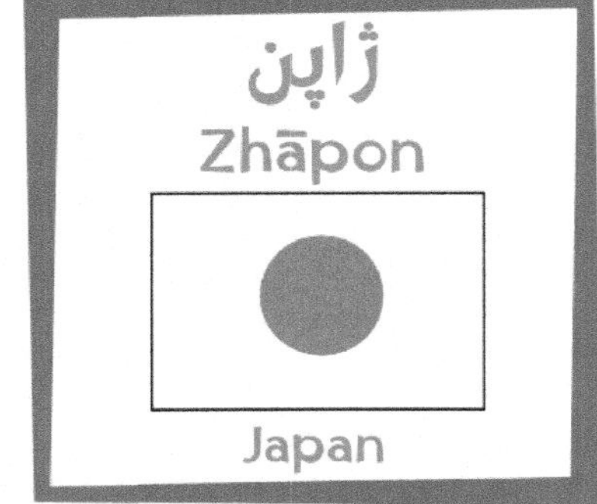
ژاپن
Zhāpon
Japan

برزیل
Berezil
Brazil

ایالت متحده
Eyālat-é Mottahedé
United States

روسیه
Rousiyé
Russia

هند
Hend
India

چین
Chin
China

کشور
KESHVAR
COUNTRY

مکزیک
Mekzik
Mexico

مصر
Mesr
Egypt

ترکیه
Torkiyé
Turkey

نیجریه
Nijeriyé
Nigeria

تایلند
Tāyland
Thailand

کره جنوبی
Koré Jonoubi
South Korea

کلمبیا
Kolombiyā
Colombia

آرژانتین
Ārzhāntin
Argentina

الجزایر
Aljazāyer
Algeria

لهستان
Lahestān
Poland

عربستان سعودی
Arabestan-é Sooudi
Saudi Arabia

کامرون
Kāmeron
Cameroon

هلند
Holand
Netherlands

سوئیس
Souis
Switzerland

سوئد
Soéd
Sweden

کشور

KESHVAR

COUNTRY

ایرلند
Irland
Ireland

بلژیک
Belzhik
Belgium

یونان
Younān
Greece

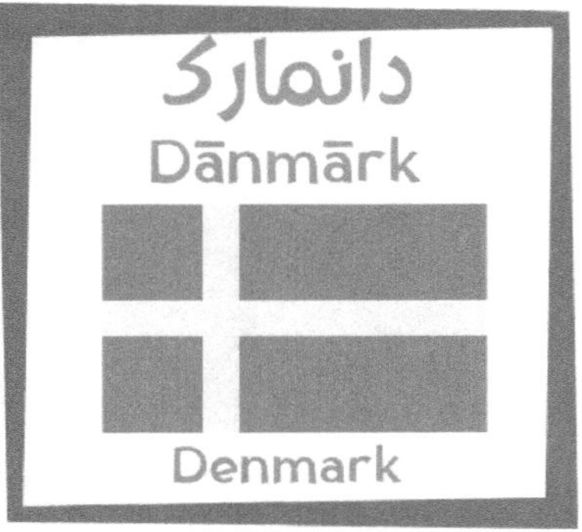
دانمارک
Dānmārk
Denmark

استرالیا
Ostorāliyā
Australia

نروژ
Norvezh
Norway

پرتقال
Porteghāl
Portugal

فنلاند
Fanlānd
Finland

اتریش
Otrish
Austria

تانزانیا
Tānzāniyā
Tanzania

اندونزی
Andonezi
Indonesia

آفریقای جنوبی
Afrighāy-é Jonoubi
South Africa

شیلی
Shili
Chile

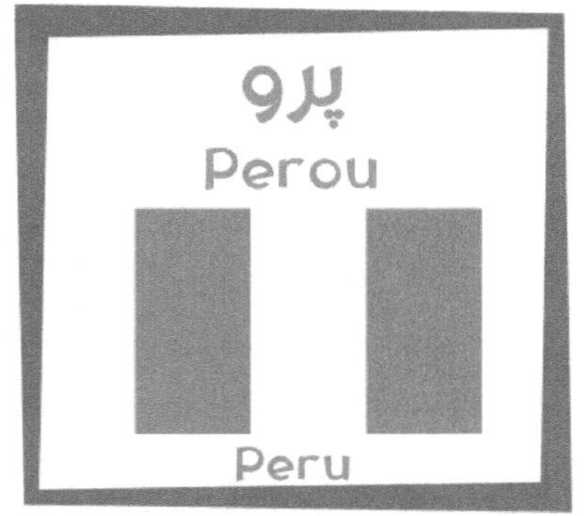
پرو
Perou
Peru

اوکراین
Okrayn
Ukraine

جمعیت
JAMĪYYAT
POPULATION

اروپایی
Oroupāyi
European

آمریکایی
Āmrikāyi
American

انگلیسی
Engelisi
DO you SPEAK English?
English

فرانسوی
Farānsavi
French

اسپانیایی
Espāniyayi
Spanish

ایتالیایی
Italiyāyi
Italien

آلمانی
Ālmāni
German

آفریقایی
Āfrighāyi
African

آسیایی
Āsiyāyi
Asian

روسی
Rousi
Russian

چینی
Chini
Chinese

کانادایی
Kānādāyi
Canadien

هندی
Hendi
Indian

برزیلی
Berzili
Brazilian

مکزیکی
Mekziki
Mexican

شلوار
Shalvār
Pants
کراوات
Kerāvāt
Tie

پیراهن
Pirāhan
Shirt
جوراب
Jourāb
Socks

کت
Kot
Jacket

عینک
Eynak
Glasses
کفش
Kafsh
Shoes
لباس
Lebās
Dress

کمربند
Kamarband
Belt
کلاه
Kolāh
Hat
binkbank
100
کیف پول
Kif-é Poul
Wallet

چتر
Chatr
Umbrella

کلاه بافتنی
Kolāh-é Bāftani
Beanie
شال گردن
Shal Gardan
Scarf
دستکش
Dastkesh
Gloves

لوازم تزئینی
lavāzemé tazini

accessories

دستبند
DASTBAND
BRACELET

ساعت
SĀAT
WATCH

جواهرآلات
JAVĀHER ĀLĀT
JEWELRY

انگشتر
ANGOSHTAR
RING

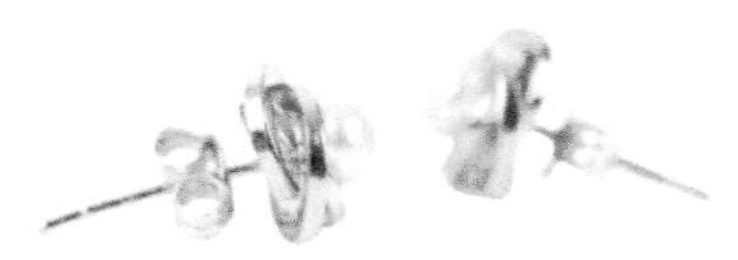

گوشواره
GOUSHVĀRÉ
EARRINGS

دستمال
DASTMĀL
HANDKERCHIEF

لباس خواب
LEBĀS KHĀB
PAJAMAS

صندل
SANDAL
SANDALS

چکمه
CHAKMÉ
BOOTS

بند کفش
BAND-É KAFSH
SHOELACE

گردنبند
GARDANBAND
NECKLACE

دمپایی
DAMPĀYI
SLIPPERS

وسایل آرایش
VASĀYEL-É ĀRĀYESH
MAKEUP

کیف دستی
KIF-É DASTI
HANDBAG

جیب
JĪB
POCKET

جهان
Jahān
Universe

کهکشان
Kahkeshān
Galaxy

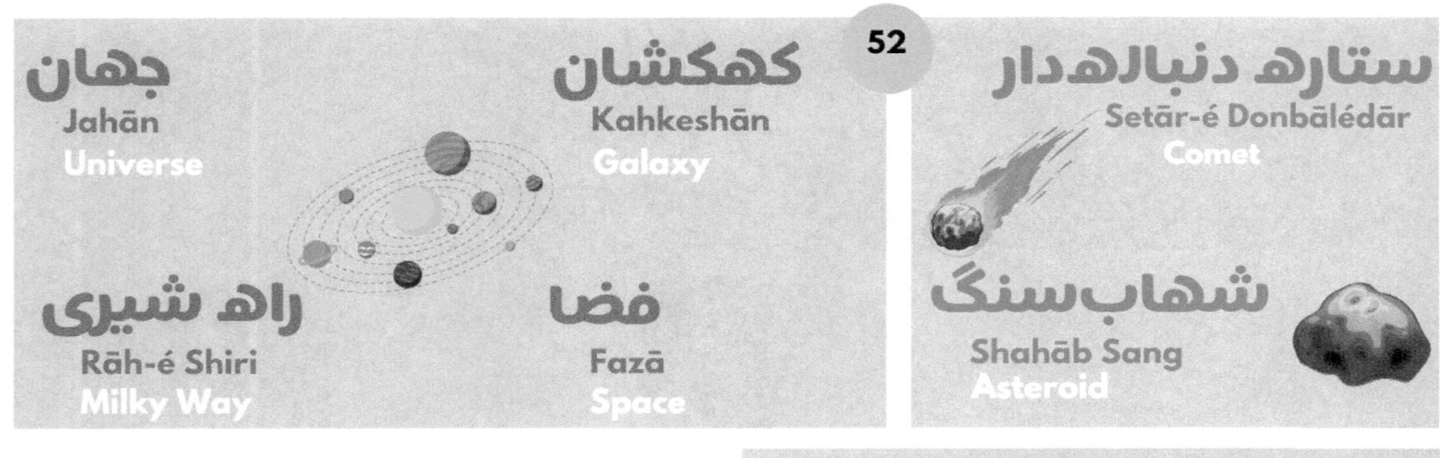

ستاره دنباله‌دار
Setār-é Donbālédār
Comet

راه شیری
Rāh-é Shiri
Milky Way

فضا
Fazā
Space

شهاب‌سنگ
Shahāb Sang
Asteroid

ماه
Māh
Moon

زمین
Zamin
Earth

ستاره
Setāré
Star

زمان
Zamān
Time

نور
Nour
Light

سیاره
Sayyāré
Planet

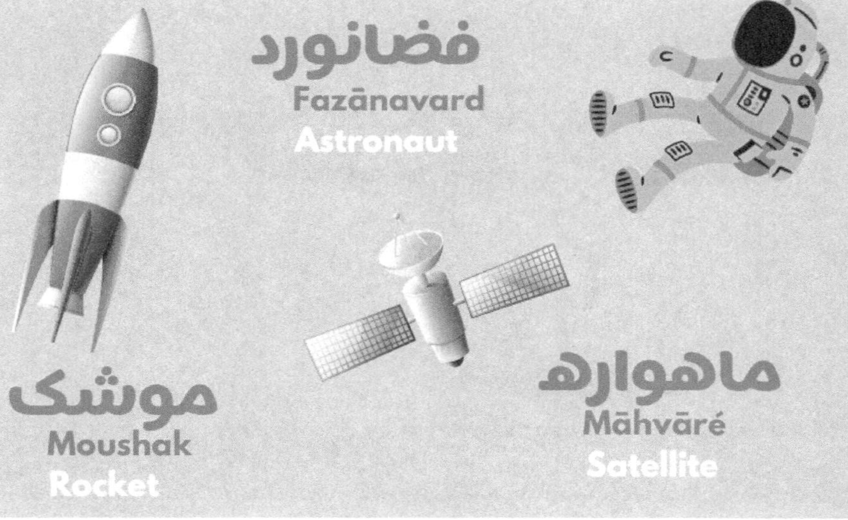

فضانورد
Fazānavard
Astronaut

موشک
Moushak
Rocket

ماهواره
Māhvāré
Satellite

قیمت
Gheymat
Price

پول
Poul
Money

پرداختن
Pardākhtan
To pay

مشتری
Moshtari
Client

هدیه
Hediyé
Gift

آنلاین
Ānlāyn
Online

بانک
Bānk
Bank

کتابفروشی
Ketābforoushi
Bookstore

داروخانه
Dāroukhāné
Pharmacy

مغازه
Maghāzé
Store

رستوران
Restourān
Restaurant

جشن
Jashn
Party

ازدواج
Ezdevāj
Wedding

تولد
Tavallod
Birth

روز تولد
Rouz-é Tavallod
Birthday

همیشه	hamishé	always
جای دیگر	jāyé digar	elsewhere
تقریباً	taghriban	approximately
همه جا	haméja	everywhere
یک جایی	yekjāyi	somewhere
هرجا	harjā	anywhere
هیچ جا	hichjā	nowhere
داخل	dākhel	inside
خارج	khārej	outside
بنابراین	banābarin	thus
نزدیک	nazdik	near
بالا	bālā	above
آهسته	āhesté	slowly
سریع	sari	quickly
واقعاً	vāghean	really

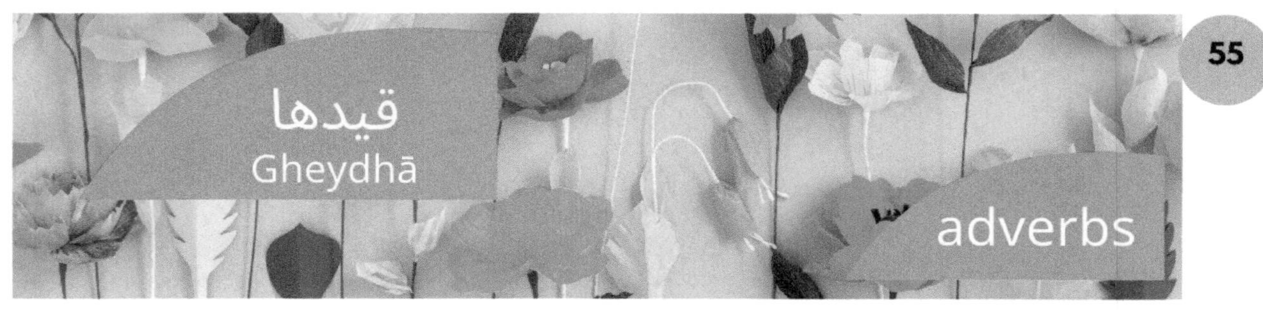

به سادگی	be sādegi	simply
به طور جدی	betoré jeddi	seriously
خوشبختانه	khoshbakhtāné	fortunately
گاهی اوقات	gāhi oghāt	sometimes
به ندرت	bé nodrat	rarely
کافی	kāfi	enough
اولاً	avalan	firstly
قبل از	ghabl az	before
بعد از	bad az	after
به هرحال	be har hāl	however
هرگز	hargez	never
اخیراً	akhiran	recently
سپس	sepas	then
اغلب	aghlab	often
معمولاً	mamolan	usually

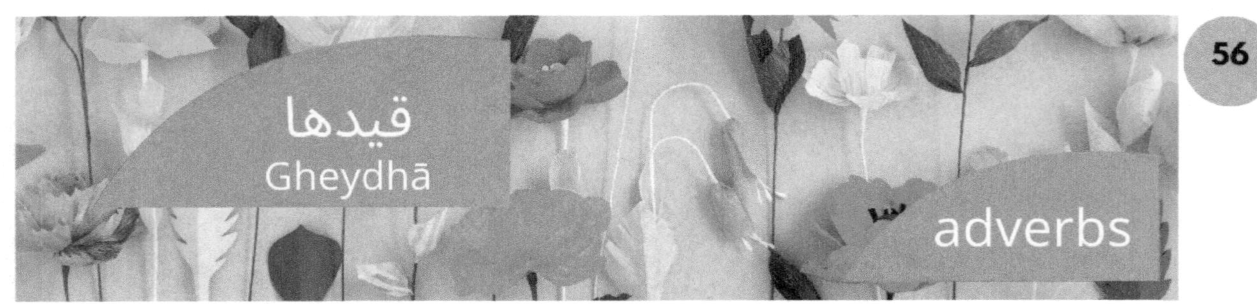

بهتر	behtar	better
به خوبی	bekhoubi	well
زیاد	ziyād	a lot
ترجیحاً	tarjihan	rather
واقعاً	vāghean	quite
پس	pas	so
همچنین	hamchenin	too
کمی	kami	little
دور	dour	far
خیلی	kheili	very
تقریباً	taghriban	almost
قبلاً	ghablan	already
از وقتیکه	az vaghtike	since
ناگهان	nāgahān	suddenly
درواقع	darvāghé	indeed

مردم mardom people

نوزاد
Nowzād
Baby

کودک
Kodak
Child

پسر
Pesar
Boy

دختر
Dokhtar
Girl

نوجوان
Nowjavān
Teenager

زن
Zan
Woman

مرد
Mard
Man

بزرگسال
Bozorgsāl
Adult

دوست
Doust
Friend

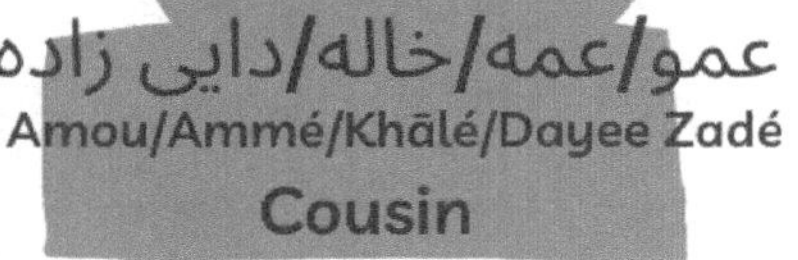
عمو/عمه/خاله/دایی زاده
Amou/Ammé/Khālé/Dayee Zadé
Cousin

همکار
Hamkār
Colleague

عشق
Eshgh
Love

دوستی
Dousti
Friendship

خوشحالی
Khoshhāli
Happiness

لذت
Lezzat
Joy

ورزش
varzesh

sport

گروه
GOROUH
TEAM

بازیکن
BĀZIKON
PLAYER

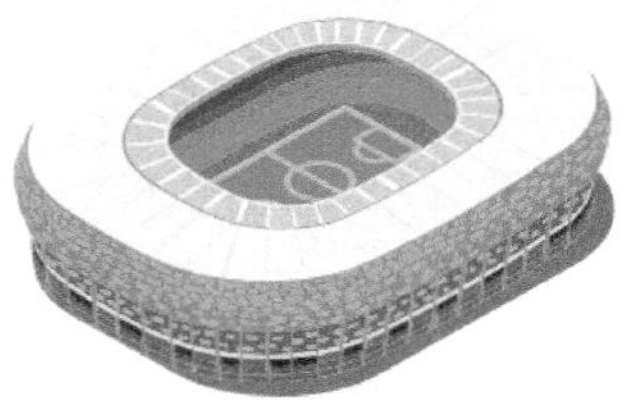

استادیوم
ESTĀDIUM
STADIUM

فوتبال
FOUTBAL
FOOTBALL/SOCCER

داور
DĀVAR
REFEREE

توپ
TOUP
BALL

پیراهن ورزشی
PIRĀHAN-É VARZESHI
JERSEY

تمرین ورزشی
TAMRINĀT-É VARZESHI
TRAINING

رتبه‌بندی
ROTBÉ BANDI
RANKING

اسب‌سواری
ASB SAVĀRI
HORSE RIDING

دوچرخه‌سواری
DOCHARKHÉ SAVĀRI
CYCLING

شنا
SHENĀ
SWIMMING

مربی
MORABBI
COACH

صدمه
SADAMÉ
INJURY

دو و میدانی
DO VA MEYDĀNI
TRACK AND FIELD

جهان
Jahān
World

رئیس جمهور
Raees Jomhour
President

حکومت
Hokoumat
Government

شهردار
Shahrdār
Mayor

سیاست
Siyāsat
Politics

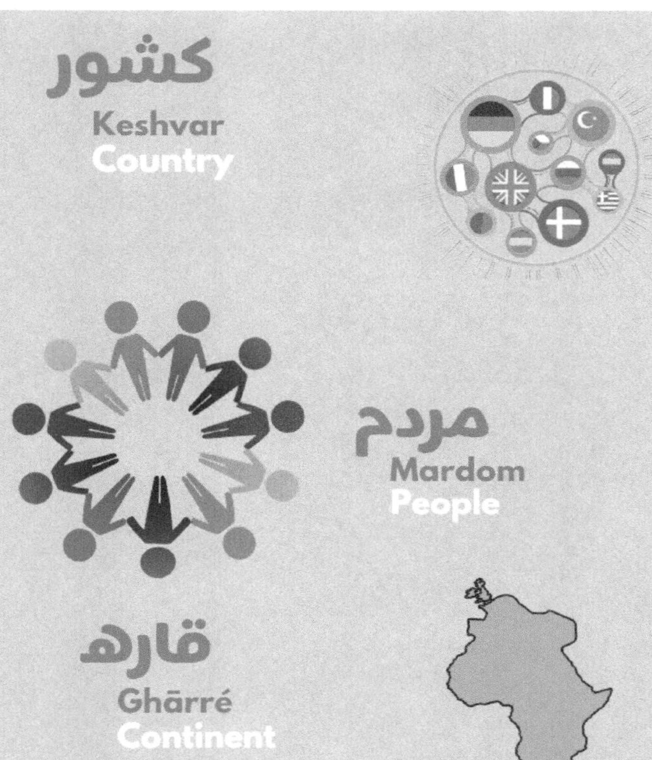

کشور
Keshvar
Country

مردم
Mardom
People

قاره
Ghārré
Continent

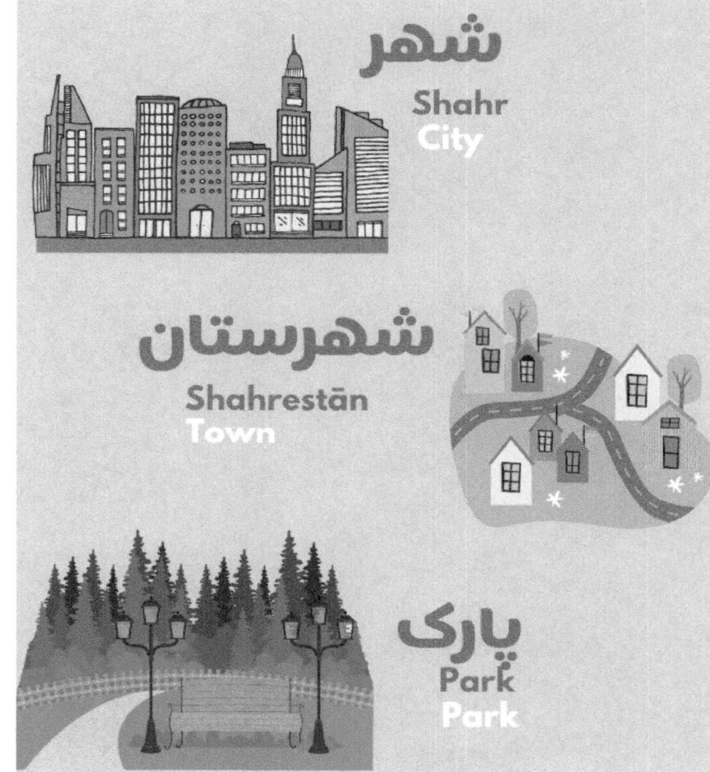

شهر
Shahr
City

شهرستان
Shahrestān
Town

پارک
Park
Park

شرکت
Sherkat
Company

جزیره
Jaziré
Island

صحرا
Sahrā
Desert

بیمارستان
Bimārestān
Hospital

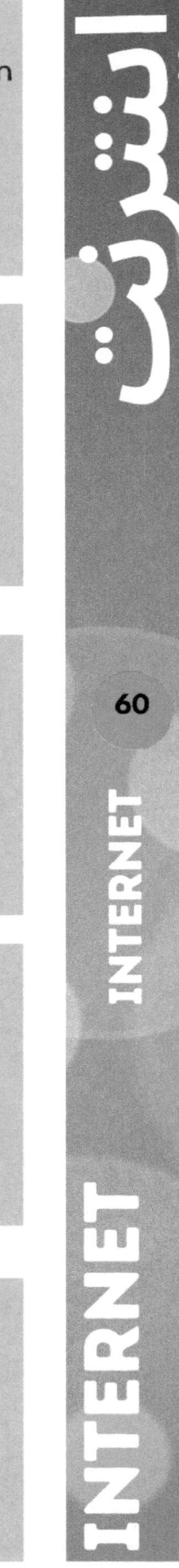

اینترنت

INTERNET

منتشر کردن
Montasher Kardan

Publish

کاربر
Kārbar

User

شبکه اجتماعی
Shabaké Ejtemāi

Social network

عضو شدن
Ozv Shodan

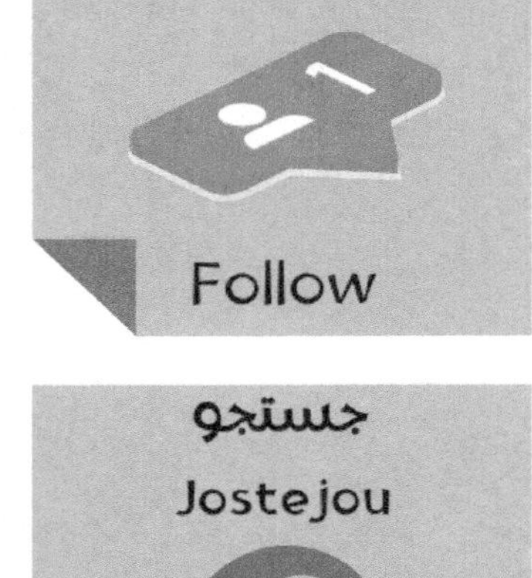

Subscribe

محتوا
Mohtavā

Content

اشتراک گذاشتن
Eshterāk Gozashtan

Share

دنبال کردن
Donbāl Kardan

Follow

آگهی
Āgahi

Advertising

خبر
Khabar

News

جستجو
Jostejou

Research

کانال
Kānāl

Channel

حساب
Hesāb

Account

لینک
Link

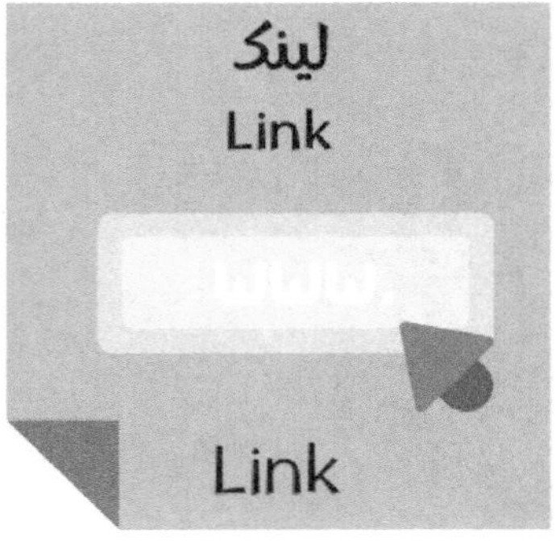

Link

گپ زدن
Gap Zadan

Chat

نظر
Nazar

Comment

اینترنت

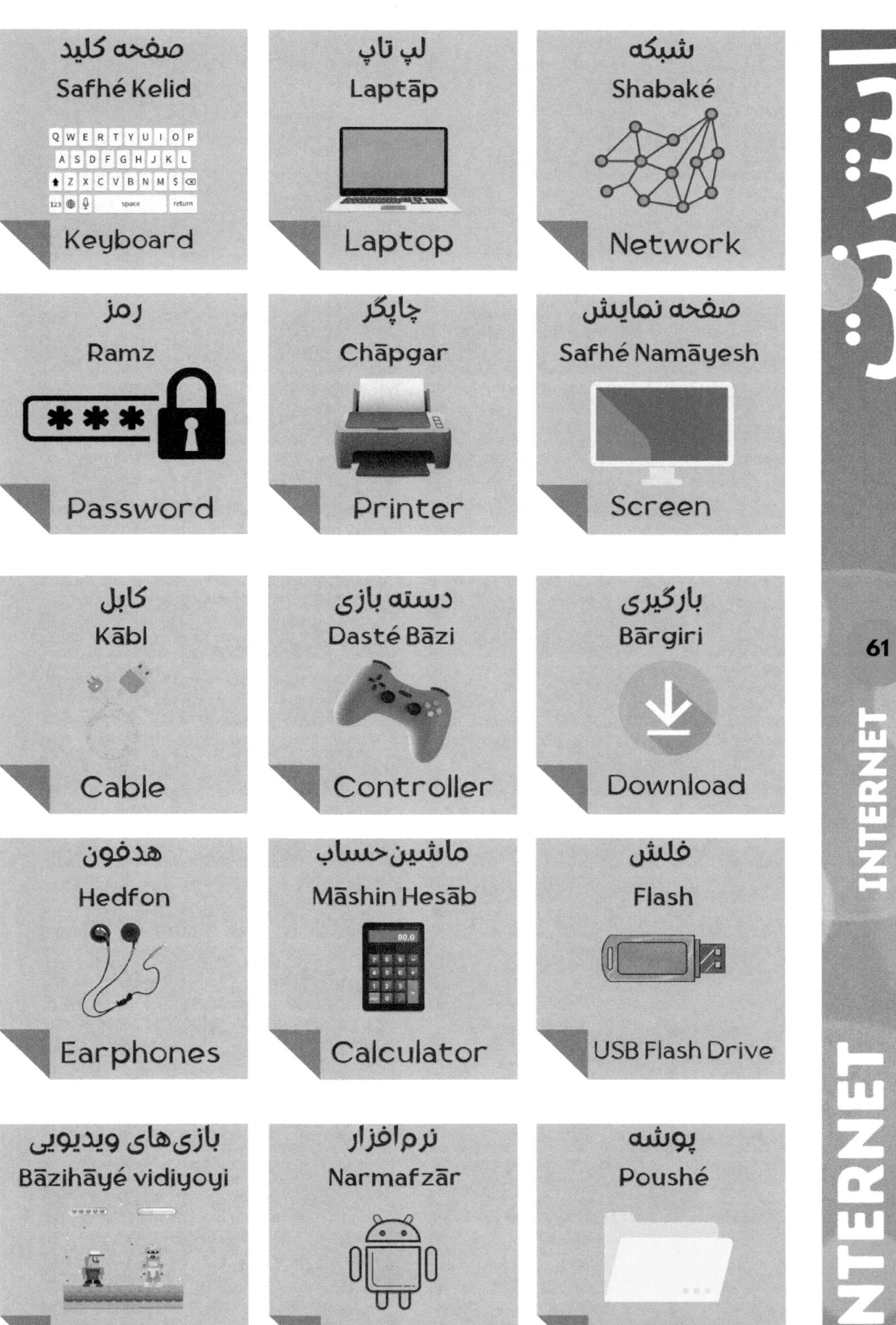

صفحه کلید
Safhé Kelid
Keyboard
لپ تاپ
Laptāp
Laptop
شبکه
Shabaké
Network
رمز
Ramz
Password
چاپگر
Chāpgar
Printer
صفحه نمایش
Safhé Namāyesh
Screen
کابل
Kābl
Cable
دسته بازی
Dasté Bāzi
Controller
بارگیری
Bārgiri
Download
هدفون
Hedfon
Earphones
ماشین حساب
Māshin Hesāb
Calculator
فلش
Flash
USB Flash Drive
بازی‌های ویدیویی
Bāzihāyé vidiyoyi
Video games
نرم افزار
Narmafzār
Software
پوشه
Poushé
File

INTERNET

مشکل	moshkel	problem
ایده	idé	idea
سوال	soāl	question
جواب	javāb	answer
فکر	fekr	thought
روح	rouh	spirit
شروع	shorou	beginning
آخر	ākhar	end
قانون	ghānoun	law
زندگی	zendegi	life
مرگ	marg	death
صلح	solh	peace
سکوت	sokout	silence
رؤیا	royā	dream
وزن	vazn	weight

عقیده	aghidé	opinion
چیز	chīz	thing
اشتباه	eshtebāh	mistake
گرسنگی	gorosnegi	hunger
تشنگی	teshnegi	thirst
انتخاب	entekhāb	choice
قدرت	ghodrat	strength
عکس	aks	picture
روبات	robāt	robot
دروغ	dorough	lie
حقیقت	haghighat	truth
سر و صدا	sar-o sedā	noise
هیچ چیز	hich chiz	nothing
همه چیز	hamé chiz	everything
نصف	nesf	half

ابزار

abzār

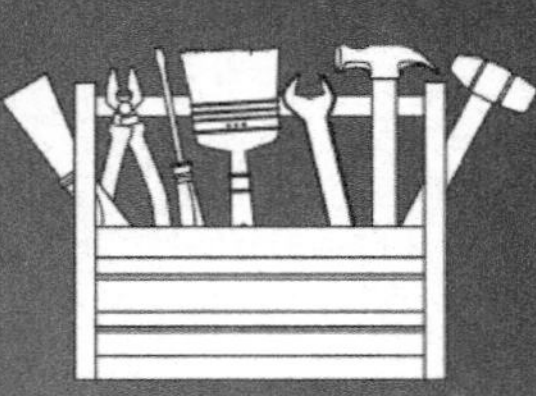

tools

تبر
TABAR
AXE

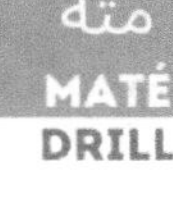

مته
MATÉ
DRILL

چسب
CHASB
GLUE

چکش
CHAKOSH
HAMMER

نردبان
NARDEBĀN
LADDER

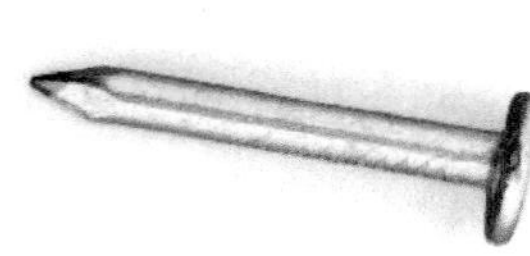

میخ
MIKH
NAIL

پیچ‌گوشتی
PICH GOUSHTI
SCREWDRIVER

چنگک
CHANGAK
RAKE

ماشین چمن‌زنی
MĀSHIN-É CHMANZANI
MOWER

اره
ARRÉ
SAW

کارتن
KARTON
CARDBOARD

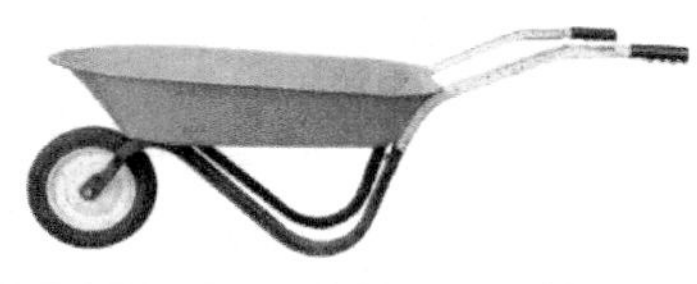

فرغون
FORGHOUN
WHEELBARROW

آب‌پاش
ĀBPASH
WATERING CAN

پیچ
PICH
SCREW

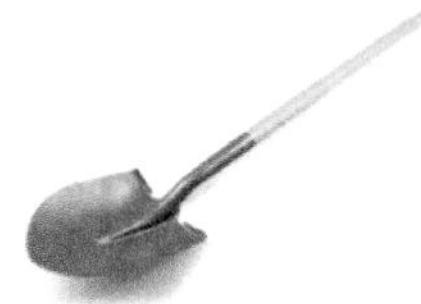

بیل
BIL
SHOVEL

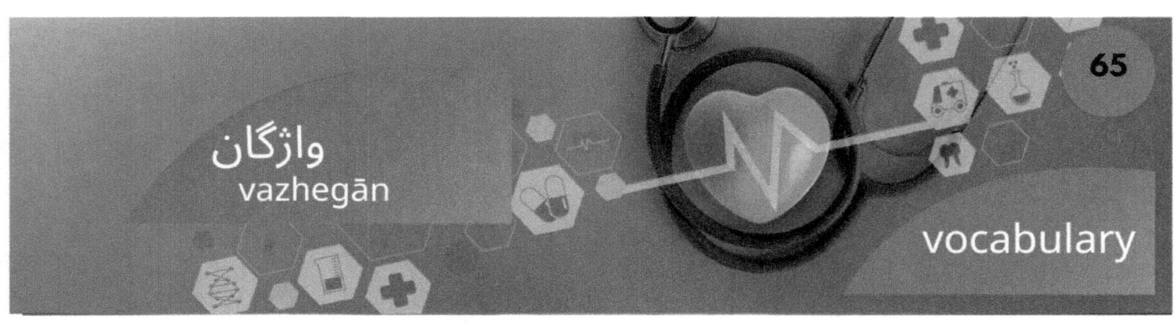

حساسیت	hassāsiyat	allergy
آنفولانزا	ānfolānzā	flu
استراحت	esterāhat	rest
دارو	dārou	medication
واکسن	vāksan	vaccine
آنتی‌بیوتیک	āntibiotik	antibiotic
تب	tab	fever
بهبود یافتن	behboud yāftan	heal
سلامتی	salāmati	health
عفونت	ofounat	infection
علامت	alāmat	symptom
واگیردار	vāgirdār	contagious
بیماری	bimāri	sickness
درد	dard	pain
سرفه	sorfé	cough

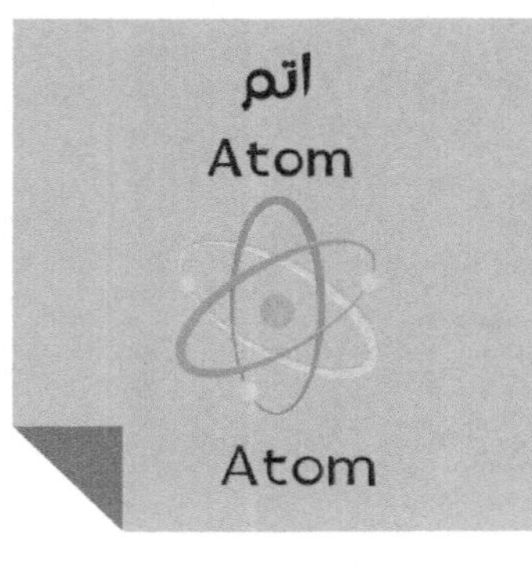
اتم
Atom
Atom

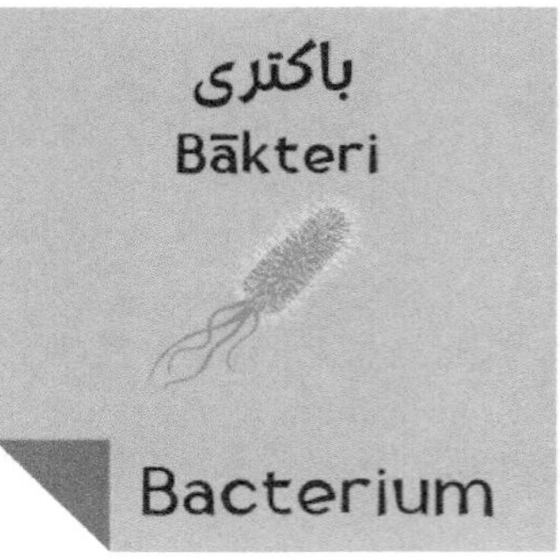
باکتری
Bākteri
Bacterium

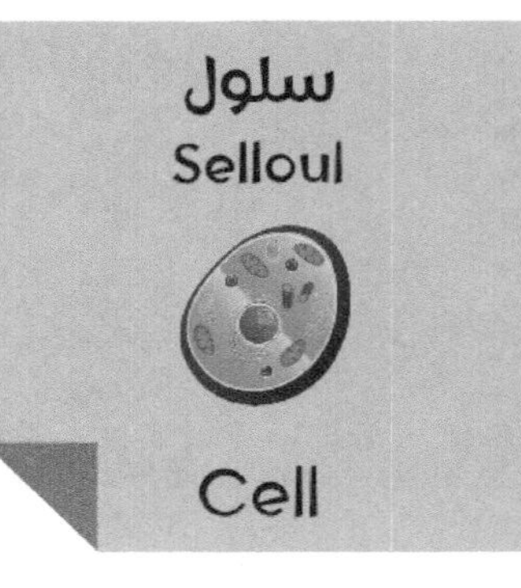
سلول
Selloul
Cell

شیمی
Shimi
Chemistry

زیست‌شناسی
Zist Shenāsi
Biology

میکروسکوپ
Mikroskop
Microscope

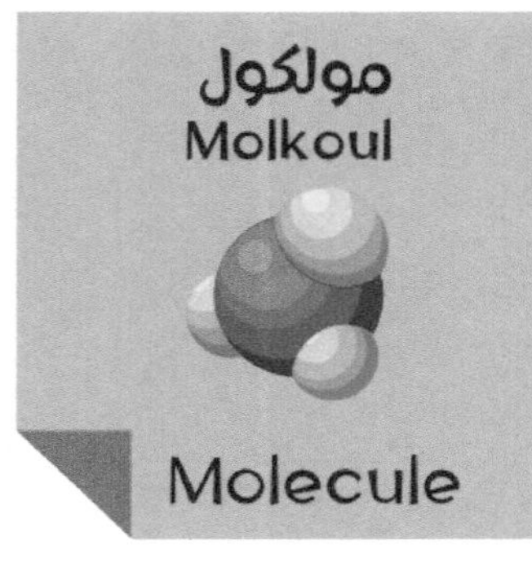
مولکول
Molkoul
Molecule

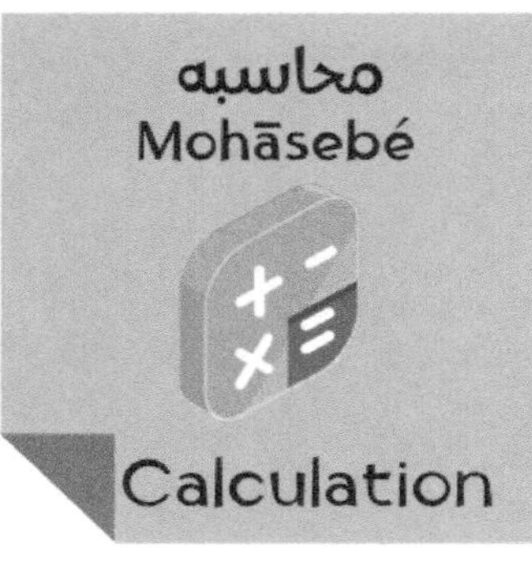
محاسبه
Mohāsebé
Calculation

نتیجه
Natijé
Result

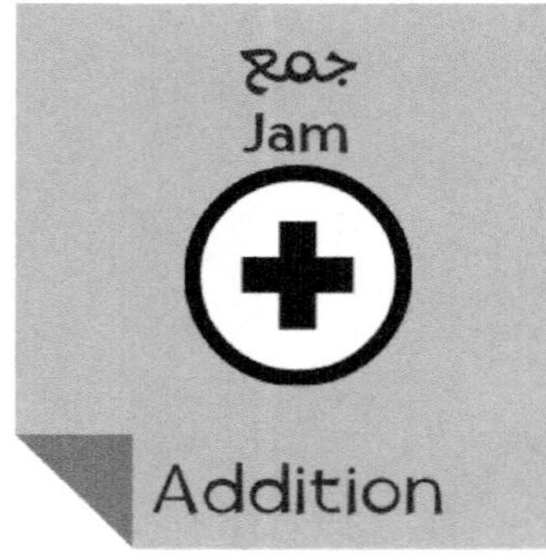
جمع
Jam
Addition

تفریق
Tafrigh
Subtraction

تقسیم
Taghsim
Division

ضرب
Zarb
Multiplication

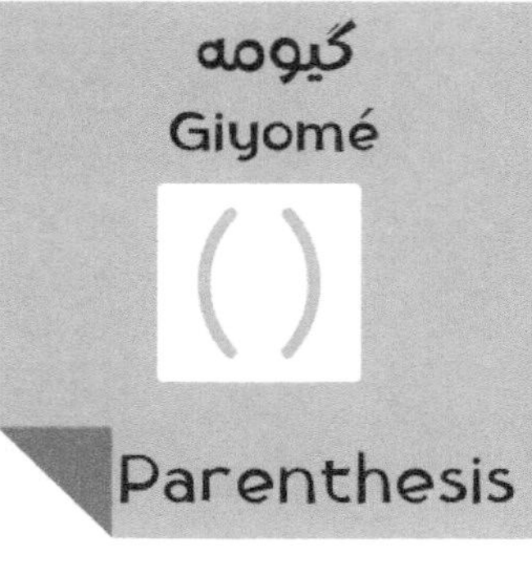
گیومه
Giyomé
Parenthesis

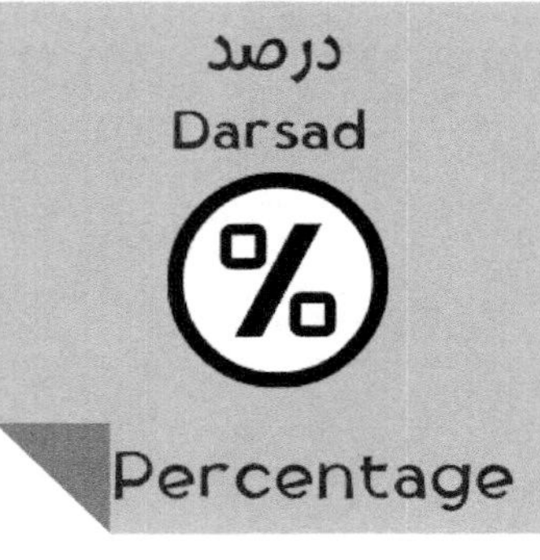
درصد
Darsad
Percentage

شهر
shahr

city

دانشگاه
DĀNESHGĀH
UNIVERSITY

کارخانه
KĀRKHĀNÉ
FACTORY

ساختمان
SĀKHTEMĀN
BUILDING

زندان
ZENDĀN
JAIL

سالن شهرداری
SĀLON-É SHAHRDĀRI
TOWN HALL

پل
POL
BRIDGE

قلعه
GHALÉ
CASTLE

قبرستان
GHABRESTĀN
CEMETERY

فواره
FAVVĀRÉ
FOUNTAIN

تونل
TOUNEL
TUNNEL

باغوحش
BAGH-É VAHSH
ZOO

دادگاه
DĀDGĀH
COURT

سیرک
SIRK
CIRCUS

کازینو
KAZINO
CASINO

آزمایشگاه
ĀZMĀYESHGĀH
LABORATORY

مصالح

MASĀLEH MATERIALS

پنبه
Panbé
Cotton

چوب
Choub
Wood

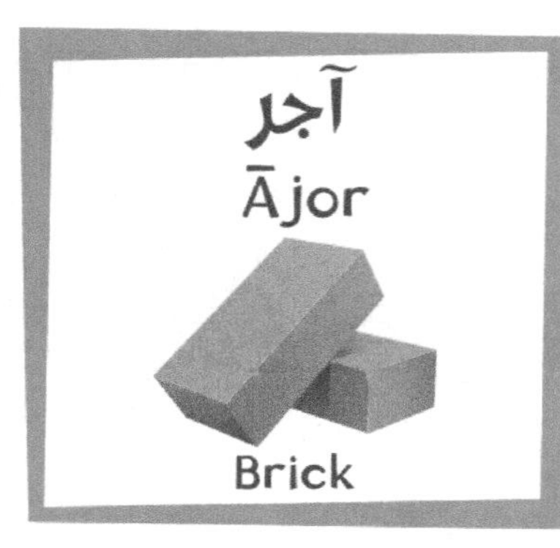
آجر
Ājor
Brick

بتون
Boton
Concrete

پشم
Pashm
Wool

چرم
Charm
Leather

فلز
Felez
Metal

مرمر
Marmar
Marble

فولاد
Foulād
Steel

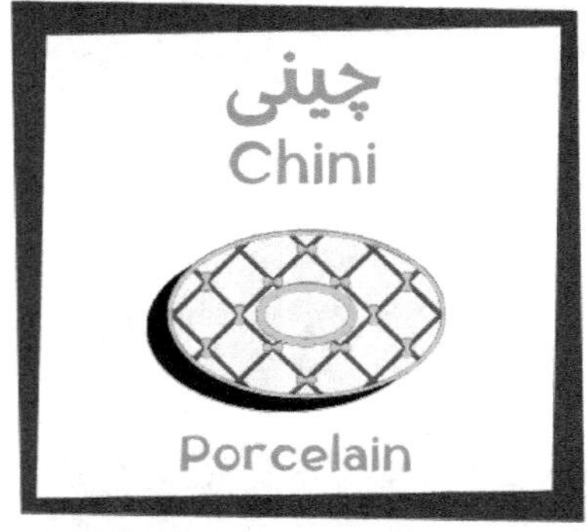
چینی
Chini
Porcelain

خاک رس
Khāk-é Ros
Clay

پلاستیک
Pelāstik
Plastic

لاستیک
Lāstik
Rubber

کاغذ
Kāghaz
Paper

شن
Shen
Sand

زمین
Zamin

Earth

زمین‌لرزه
zamin larzé
earthquake

آتش
ātash
fire

مزرعه
mazraé
field

بهمن
bahman
avalanche

گردباد
gerdbād
tornado

پرتگاه
partgāh
cliff

اقیانوس
oghyānous
ocean

آتشفشان
atashfeshān
volcano

تپه‌شنی
tappé Sheni
dune

موج
mowj
wave

تپه
tappé
hill

کوه یخی
kouh-é yakhi
glacier

جنگل
jangal
jungle

دره
darré
valley

غار
ghār
cave

موسیقی
mousighi

ارکست
ORKEST
ORCHESTRA

آهنگ
ĀHANG
SONG

نوازنده
NAVĀZANDÉ
MUSICIAN

گیتار
GITĀR
GUITAR

خواننده
KHĀNANADÉ
SINGER

پیانو
PIYANO
PIANO

طبل
TABL
DRUMS

ویولن
VIYALON
VIOLIN

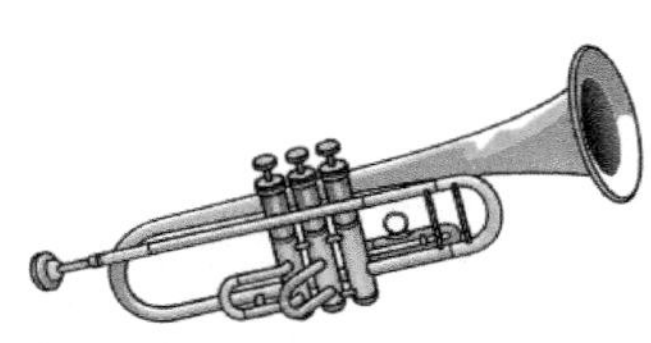

شیپور
SHEYPOUR
TRUMPET

متن ترانه
MATN-É TARĀNÉ
LYRICS

تماشاگر
TAMĀSHĀGAR
AUDIENCE

صدا
SEDĀ
VOICE

بلندگو
BOLANDGOU
MICROPHONE

صحنه
SAHNÉ
STAGE

حجم
HAJM
VOLUME

آدرس
Ādres
Address

پاکت نامه
Pākat-é Nāmé
Envelope

صندوق پستی
Sandough-é Posti
Mailbox

پست
Post
Mail

تمبر
Tambar
Stamp

صورتحساب
Sourat Hesāb
Bill

الکتریسیته
Elekterisité
Electricity

گاز
Gāz
Gas

حقوق
Hoghough
Salary

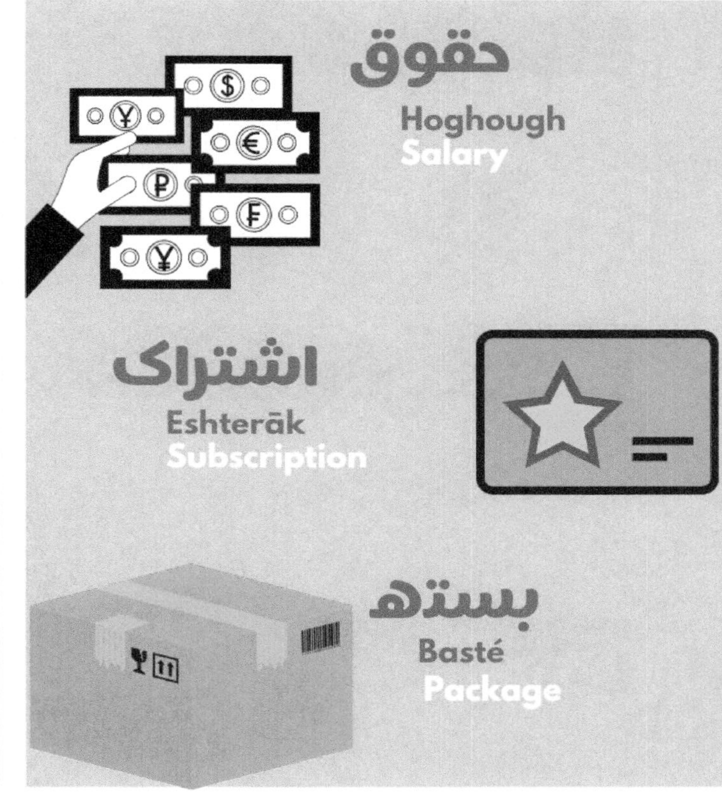

اشتراک
Eshterāk
Subscription

بسته
Basté
Package

پستچی
Postchi
Postman

فرستادن
Ferestādan
Send

خریدن
Kharidan
Buy

فروختن
Foroukhtan
Sell

زیست‌بوم شناسی
zist boum shenāsi
ecology

بازیافت
BĀZYĀFT
RECYCLE

محیط زیست
MOHIT-É ZIST
ENVIRONMENT

آلودگی
ĀLOUDEGI
POLLUTION

آفت‌کش
ĀFAT KOSH
PESTICIDES

طبیعی
TABIEE
ORGANIC

گیاهخوار
GIHĀH KHĀR
VEGETARIAN

انرژی
ENERZHI
ENERGY

زغال‌سنگ
ZOGHĀL SANG
COAL

بنزین
BENZIN
GASOLINE

هسته‌ای
HASTEIEE
NUCLEAR

زیست‌بوم
ZIST BOUM
ECOSYSTEM

پوشش جانوری
POUSHESH-É JĀNEVARI
FAUNA

پوشش گیاهی
POUSHESH-É GIYĀHI
FLORA

دما
DAMĀ
TEMPERATURE

قطب
GHOTB
ARCTIC

Olwyn's Treasured Samplers

By Olwyn Horwood

Publisher's Note

The designs in this book were made using fabric and threads available in retail shops in New Zealand. As publisher, we are aware that some of these items may not be found in your local shop, so every effort has been made to include and suggest alternative materials that can be found in your country. We know that the alternatives suggested will give very satisfactory results and most importantly in the end, your own masterpieces to enjoy! As always we welcome your letters, email messages and telephone calls. The messages we receive from everywhere needlework is enjoyed brighten our day. Please let us know your progress with these samplers.
Prue Georgeson

Published by Georgeson Publishing Limited

P.O. Box 100-667, North Shore Mail Centre
Auckland, New Zealand
Ph: 649 410 2079 Fax: 649 410 2069
Email: gpl@georgeson.co.nz Web site: www.georgeson.co.nz

ISBN NO 09 582 10586

Editor: Prue Georgeson
Photography: Maria Sainsbury
Illustrations and Layout: Andreena Buckton of Noodle Design
Printed: New Zealand

CONTENTS

Introduction

These three samplers are individual pieces stitched at different times. They are a continuation of my joy in stitching samplers, a joy I know I share with many others. Selecting samplers to include in this book was not easy but these three samplers were the most frequently asked for designs after the publication of *Blue Ribbon Sampler*. Each of the three is special to me in a different way.

The Adam and Eve Sampler was stitched because I realized I didn't have one of this genre, which has enjoyed a long period of popularity, in my collection. It is the earliest of the biblical motifs featuring human figures that appeared on English samplers, first appearing at the beginning of the eighteenth century and becoming quite common in the latter half of that century.

The Pomegranate Sampler is made up of a selection of pomegranate designs from my collection. The pomegranate is part of our cultural history, first mentioned in Greek mythology when Persephone ate its seeds when held captive in the underworld. The pomegranate is mentioned in the Old Testament and has symbolic meaning in modern Christianity. It is also a most interesting fruit which is represented in many different designs.

The Double Band Sampler was inspired by a sampler with a similar layout that I originally saw in *Historical Embroideries* by Louisa Pesel. I am always interested in samplers which are different from those I have seen before, be it the layout, choice of colours, stitches used or a combination of these things. I thought this sampler was unusual and for that reason it inspired me.

Verse for a wedding sampler

Henceforth you go down
life's pathway together,
and may the Father
of all mercies
bind you together in
true love
and faithfulness and
grant you his blessing.

I always enjoy planning and designing samplers. I decide on the theme and which pattern designs I will include. These decisions both influence and are influenced by the size of the piece of fabric I wish to use, its weave, thread count and colour and the colours of the threads with which I would like to stitch. In samplers featuring bands of pattern I always select the bands to appear across the base of the sampler first and work up. This is because, to my mind, the bottom band is the most important band as it is where we unconsciously focus when we first look at a sampler. The bottom band has to form the anchor for the rest of the sampler, it gives balance and is generally the widest band stitched with the deeper shades of the colours used.

When I have stitched approximately one half to two thirds of the area I select the pattern for the top of the Sampler. This enables me to ensure that the Sampler will be visually balanced and pleasing to the eye. Subsequent patterns are then selected to complete the design. I never work out the complete design of the Sampler before I start stitching. There must always be opportunity for spontaneous changes. I find it more interesting to make changes as I go along.

I enjoyed designing and stitching these samplers. I always do. I wish you equal pleasure in stitching them.

Olwyn Horwood,
February 2002,
Auckland, New Zealand.

Requirements

Verse 1816 sampler

Let the mind your noblest thoughts engage
Its beauties last beyond the flight of ages

Linen

The best fabric for cross stitch and samplers is beautiful, evenweave linen. It is a fabric that has been used to make samplers for hundreds of years. It is long lasting and is not attractive to moths and similar thread-eating insects. It has stood the test of time and when stitching these beautiful designs that take many hours to create it is important to buy materials worthy of your time and effort in creating, what will be, a masterpiece and heirloom for generations to come.

When you buy the linen for these samplers take the time to check that it is woven in such a way that there is a gap between each thread. This will make your counting so much easier. Two linens can have the same thread count but be woven quite differently giving one a dense appearance and the other an open appearance with threads that can be individually counted quite easily. The latter linen is the one to choose for working samplers like these. There are many suitable linens available. Check the fabrics available at your favourite needlework store and choose a linen that you personally find easy to count and with a thread count you enjoy working with as you will be spending many hours working with it. Fabric quantities are given for linen with a thread count of 28 - 35 threads per inch for each sampler. All of these linens will create a sampler that will give you lasting satisfaction and pride.

If you are unable to buy the linen mentioned in the requirements do not be concerned. There is a wide range of alternative linens that can be used most satisfactorily. If you are uncertain which shade of linen to buy, select the threads to be used and hold them against the linens you are considering. This will make the choice much easier. You will find that against some linens the threads will 'glow' while against other linens the overall appearance is 'dull'.

Threads

To create each of these samplers different colour palettes were used. The Adam and Eve Sampler was stitched on natural linen which influenced my choice of rich blues and coral tones - these are enhanced and highlighted by the linen. The colours used for the Pomegranate Sampler were inspired by the pomegranate itself and the linen. Variations of the colour of the fruit and its seeds were combined with yellow toned greens, which look superb on 'tea dyed' linen. The Double Band Sampler was worked on a pale blue shaded linen, with 31 threads to the inch using a large palette of approximately 30 different colours. This gives variety yet ensures that different designs within the sampler blend together well. I find it easier to work successfully in the middle range of colours than to work with all dark or all light tones.

All these samplers were stitched using DMC and Anchor stranded cotton threads. The numbers for these threads plus Au Ver a Soie silk threads are given.

All our talents increase
in the using,
And every faculty, both
good and bad,
Strengthens by exercise.

Anne Bronte
1820-1849

Threads for Cross Stitch

I recommend using one thread of stranded cotton for all cross stitch when working on linen with 28 - 35 threads to the inch. One thread of stranded cotton gives a fine antique look to the sampler but if you feel you would like a heavier look work a test sample on the edge of the linen using two threads of stranded cotton and then beside it work a test block using one thread of stranded cotton. Choose the stitching with the effect you find most pleasing. I used one thread of stranded cotton when stitching these samplers.

Needles

The needle, the embroidery thread and the thread of the fabric to be embroidered should be of the same thickness. A tapestry needle is best to work with as it does not split the threads of the fabric you are embroidering. The size of the needles to use with the different counts of linen are:

Threads per inch	*Tapestry needle size*
28	24
30-32	26
35	28

Scissors

A pair of small sharp pointed scissors, kept purely for cutting threads, is required.

Frames

A small round wooden frame is best for using with this embroidery. I recommend one from 10cm (4") to 18 cm (7"). My personal favourite is 15 cm or 6" across the inner ring. It is important to wrap the inner ring with bias binding to soften the strain on the material while it is being held in the frame. Do not have the frame 'drum tight' or so tight that it marks the linen or stitching. I 'sew stitch' all cross stitch (for more information on 'sew stitch' see page 9).

I expect to pass through
this world but once;
Any good thing therefore
that I can do
Or any kindness that I
can show to any
fellow-creature,
Let me do it now;
Let me not defer
or neglect it,
For I shall not pass
this way again.

Grellett Stephen
1773-1855

Charts

Each square on every chart in this book represents two threads of fabric. The shaded area on the charts indicates where the chart overlaps the chart from the previous page.
The charts all overlap so that movement from one chart to the next is easy. The threads assigned to each symbol change with each Sampler. This will make it easier to follow individual charts.

Requirements for the individual samplers are given at the start of the instructions for each sampler, see page 22 for the Adam and Eve Sampler, page 32 for the Pomegranate Sampler and page 56 for the Double Band Sampler.

Stitching Techniques

Before you Begin

All evenweave linen will fray easily when handled. To avoid this oversew all raw edges before starting your embroidery. Use a fine sewing machine thread matching the colour of the linen so that the edging can be left on when the hem is turned in. If a heavy thread is used it may show through the hem or cause an uneven ridge. Use a three stitch zig zag, serpentine stitch or whatever variation your machine has which does not have long stitches as these may shrink and pull when your masterpiece is given a wash.

Sewing Methods

There are two different methods of sewing the different stitches in these samplers.

Stab Stitch - in this method of sewing there are two movements - the needle is taken from the front to the back in one movement and then from the back to the front in a second separate movement. This method is more generally used for work in large frames, canvas, tapestry, some parts of gold work, stump work and crewel work but is also used by some for satin and cross stitch.

Sew Stitch - this is my favoured method of sewing cross and satin stitches. It is ideal to use when work does not have to be held very tightly in a frame. A 'rounder' stitch is formed and it is also a lot quicker as there is only one movement rather than the two used in 'stab' stitch.

How to Start

Anchoring under subsequent stitches - There are a number of different ways of starting your thread. A simple method, possibly for the more experienced stitcher, is to leave a 2 - 3cm (1-1 1/2") length of thread which is then anchored under subsequent stitching.

Surface method - If you are a beginner you may find it easier to leave a length of thread on the surface of the material to be finished later. To do this take your needle from the front to the back of the work, approximately 5cm (2") away from where you plan to start stitching, leaving a 5cm (2") length of thread on top of the fabric. Start to stitch and when you have covered some distance the thread on top of your work is taken to the back and finished into your stitching (fig 1).

fig 1

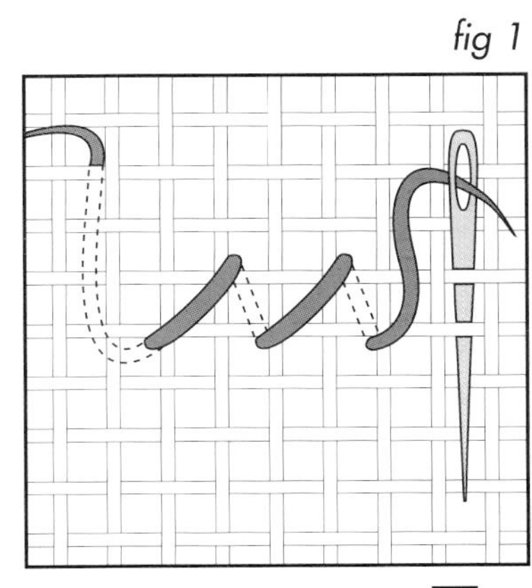

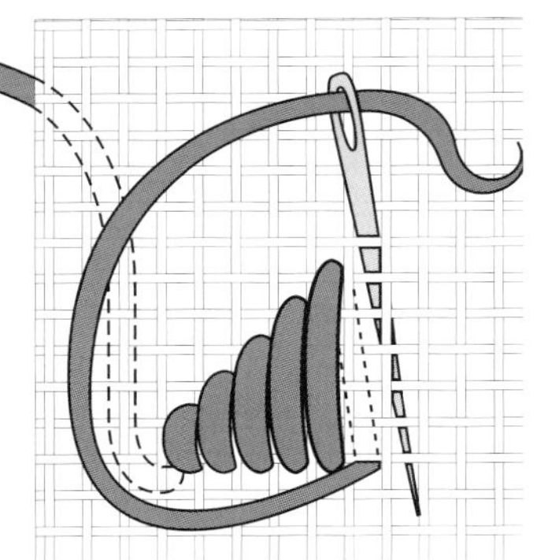
fig 2

Back Stitch - When you are working satin stitch you can work a couple of little back stitches in an area that will later be covered by the satin stitch.

Long Thread Method - Another handy tip is to use an extra long thread. Start stitching with half the length of thread, use up all the thread working one way, then rethread your needle with the remaining length of thread, turn your work around and work in the other direction. This is particularly useful for satin stitch and the stems in cross stitch designs (fig 2).

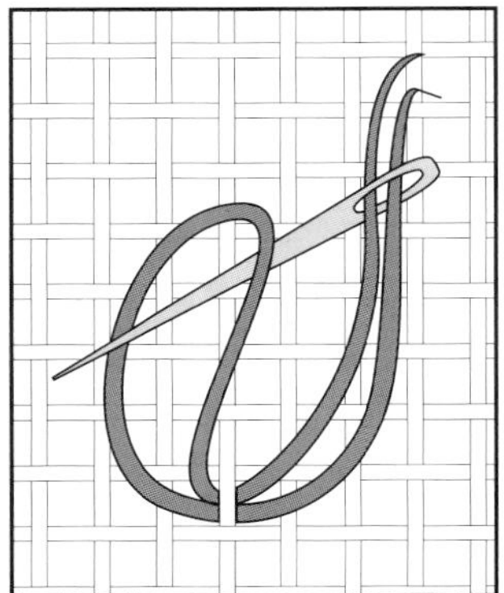
fig 3

Loop Method – Very useful when you are using a double thread. Take one long length of thread, fold in half and thread the cut ends through the eye of the needle. Start stitching in the correct position as shown on the chart, taking the needle under one thread, then thread the needle through the loop, now stitch the design following the chart (fig 3). Neat and quick without a knot in sight.

Threading a needle when working with just one thread

This is a most convenient way to thread a needle when working with just one thread. Cut a 46cm (18") length of thread. Fold it 10cm (4") from one end to form a loop, thread this loop through the eye of the needle then take the loop down over the point of the needle and pull tight (fig 4). You will have no problems with your needle coming unthreaded. (A very handy way to stitch with rayon threads also.)

fig 4

Finishing

At the back of your work take the needle under your stitching for about 2cms (3/4 of an inch), do a little slip or half knot then thread the needle back the 2cms and cut.

Whip the thread end up a row of stitches rather than across for a tidier finish (fig 5).

When no specific instructions are given for starting and finishing it is presumed you will use one of the methods given above.

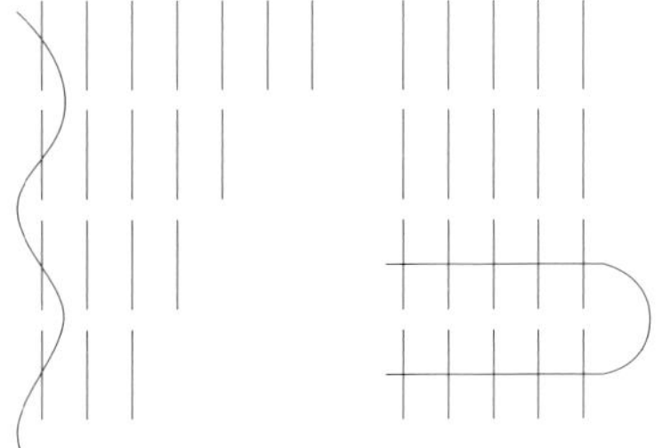
fig 5

Cross Stitch

Cross stitch was known to the ancient Egyptians and was such an important part of everyday lives that embroidery frames were put into the tombs of aristocratic ladies. Cross stitch patterns can be found in most of the different cultures of the world from Egypt and Iran to the Balkans and in countries throughout Europe. It is found decorating christening shawls, cradle covers, trousseau bed linen, altar cloths and clerical robes.

Where to Start Stitching

Start where a vertical thread is lying on top of the horizontal thread, marked A, see fig. 1

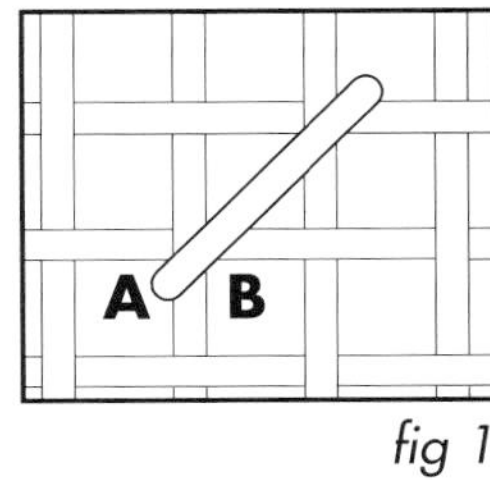

fig 1

With the first stitch starting where a vertical thread is lying on top of the horizontal thread, as shown, all following stitches will start in the same position throughout your embroidery. As well as making a neater stitch it is a most useful check. If you come to start a new stitch and it is beside a horizontal thread (marked B) you instantly know that somewhere you have sewn over one or three threads, not two. Check as you sew and also at the start of the return row when working a long line of stitches.

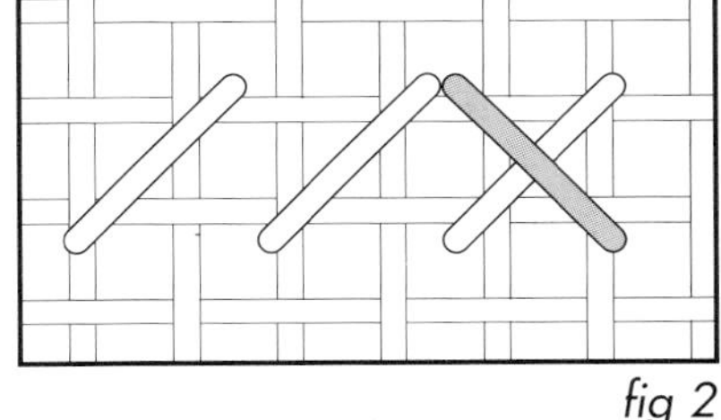
fig 2

Always work the first stitch from left to right and the second stitch right to left, fig. 2. For a professional finish all cross stitches must have the top diagonal thread lying in the same direction.

When you are stitching you may find it easier to work in a certain area or follow a particular pattern if you turn your work around. If you have worked the first half of some of your stitches and then decide the angle is not comfortable turn your work 180 degrees and you will see the first half of your cross stitch is still lying left to right so that you can happily continue your stitching at the new angle. Do not turn your work 90 or 270 degrees as this will cause irregularities in the way your stitching lies.

fig 1

Counted Satin Stitch also known as Geometric Satin Stitch

This is a stitch with lots of possibilities. The basic satin stitch dates back to ancient times and many variations of the stitch have developed over the centuries. The stitch may be left flat against the fabric or pulled tight depending on the effect required. It may be worked in blocks or to create a pattern.

The stitches should lie adjacent to each other without overlapping. The thread should be kept evenly twisted throughout the work by turning the needle in the fingers when necessary. Each stitch should lie flat on the fabric and should not 'pull' the threads out of position. It is stitched using a tapestry needle. A laying tool can be useful when working satin stitch to achieve a really smooth finished stitch. Satin stitch may be worked in either the 'stab' stitch or 'sew stitch' method. For more information on these two methods of sewing see page 9.

To Start

Satin stitch is usually worked in blocks and this makes it very easy to start - just work a couple of little back stitches in an area that will later be covered by the satin stitch or use the Loop Method (page 10.)

To Finish

Take your needle through to the back of your work, slip it under the stitching for a short distance, do a little slip knot and then take the needle under the stitching for a further distance.

Square Eyelet

Always start at the outside of the eyelet and take the needle down in the centre. Work around in sequence following the diagram (fig 1). All even numbers are in the centre. I find it easier to start in the corner.

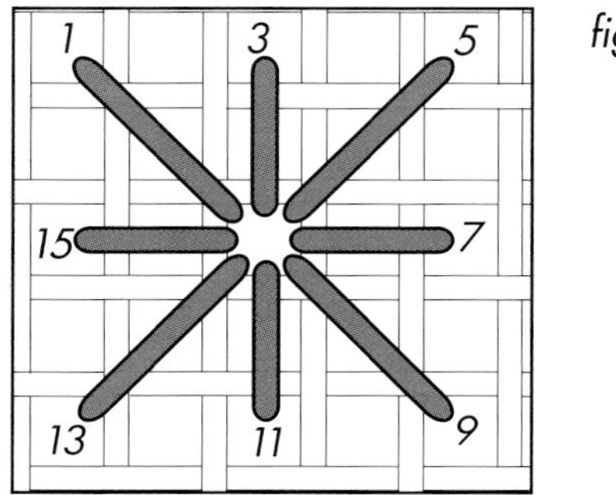

fig 1

All even numbers are in the centre

Holbein Stitch

Holbein stitch is worked in running stitch in two journeys using a tapestry needle. It is important to keep the thread tension even. In the first journey the stitches are evenly spaced leaving gaps to be filled in on the return journey (fig. 1).

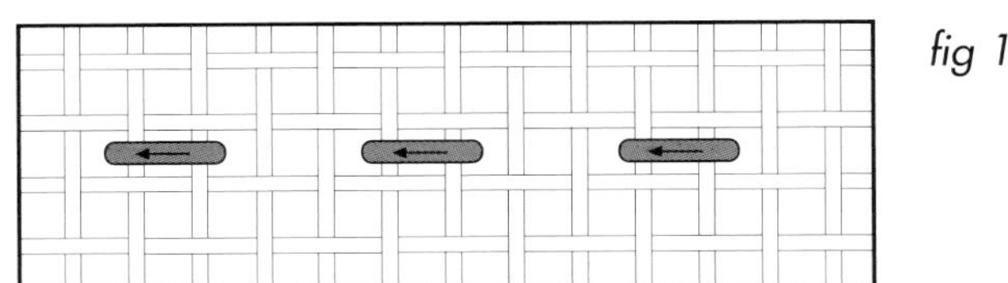

fig 1

HANDY HINT
Always neaten fabric edges before you begin to stitch.

To work the second journey turn the work around 180° so as to continue working from right to left There are different methods you can choose for working the return journey but the method I find most satisfactory is to bring my needle up through the fabric above the thread of the first journey and then go down below it (fig. 2).

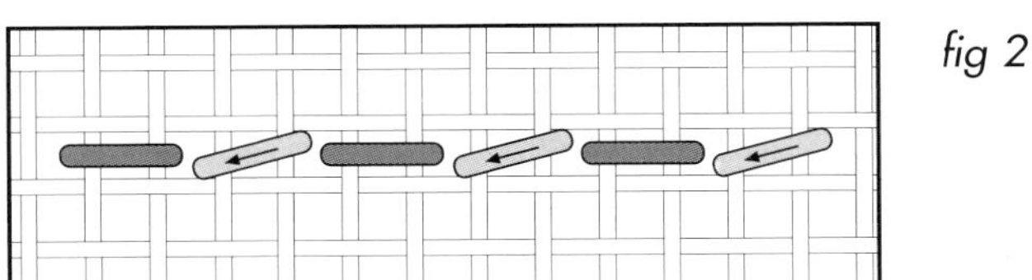

fig 2

After adjusting the thread tension your stitches will line up as shown (fig. 3).

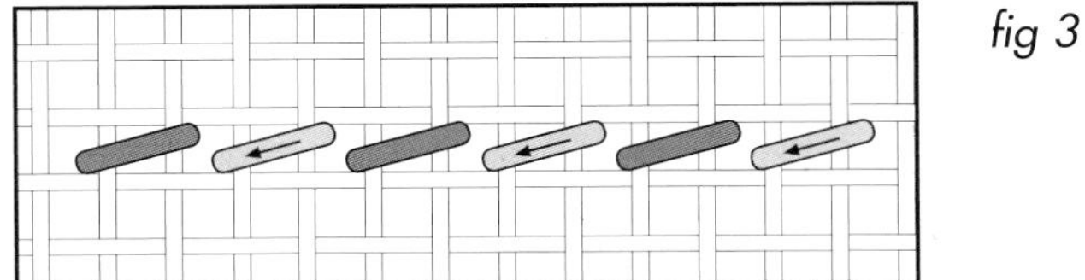

fig 3

Antique Hem Stitch

This method of hem stitching is usually used to secure a hem or give a firm edge after one or two threads (or number required) have been withdrawn. The number of threads to be withdrawn varies according to the fabric used and type of work. On very fine fabrics only a few threads are withdrawn whilst more threads must be withdrawn for wide borders suitable for sheets and tablecloths. Stitch using a fine tapestry needle to avoid splitting the threads. This stitch is used to secure the hem of the Double Band Sampler.

HANDY HINT
Use the right size needle for the work.

Working from left to right hold your work with the folded edge of the hem against your body and the hem facing you. Bring the needle up two threads down from the folded edge of the hem, take the needle to the right pass it behind four threads of fabric at the edge of the hem (fig 1). Next take the needle between the fabric and the hem (beside your first stitch) bring it through the hem two threads down as before (fig 2). Continue in this way.

fig 1

Note: one thread has been withdrawn

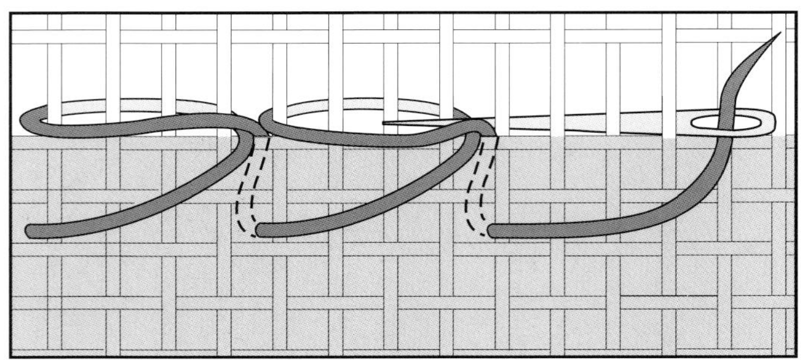

fig 2

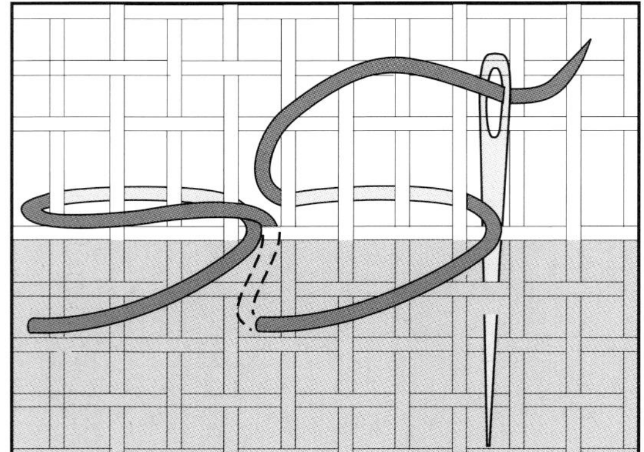

Scandinavian Edging Stitch

This is a simple, light, but very durable edging stitch. It is a pulled thread stitch and tension on the thread while stitching helps to create the lacy texture. It is actually two stitches worked in two separate stages. The first is stem stitch which is worked on the wrong side of the fabric. It is stitched using a heavier thread and often in a contrasting colour, to create an interesting textured edge. In the second stage an edging stitch is worked.

"After many years of experimenting with different weights of thread I have found that a Perle 8 thread is perfect for material with 25 - 30 threads to the inch, for finer fabric with 31-35 threads to the inch Perle 12 is better."

Stage I - *Stem Stitch - work on the wrong side of the fabric*

When working the stem stitch it is important to use a slightly heavier thread than is used for the rest of your stitching so that a 'picot', big enough to be seen as part of the edging, is created. If the thread is too fine the 'picot' will disappear into the fabric and be lost between the stitches. However the thread must be fine enough to enable you to work the second row of stitching comfortably.

For clarity the stitch is worked over four threads in the illustrations but it can be worked over three threads if you prefer.

1. Start in your preferred starting method and begin the first row of stitching - the stem stitch, *working on the wrong side of the fabric*. Bring your needle up in the correct position. Take one stitch over four threads working from left to right (fig 1).

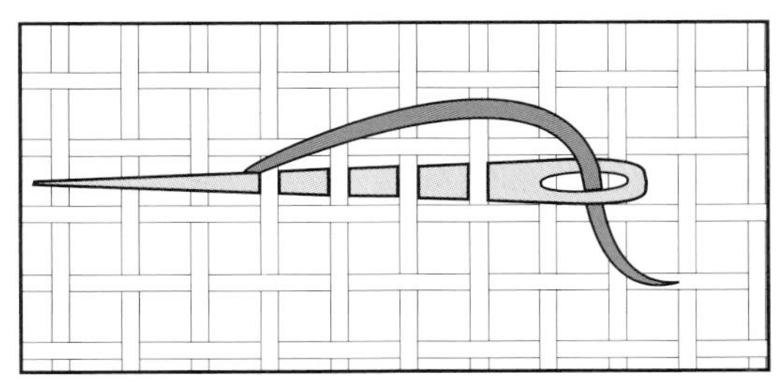

fig 1

2. Take the next stitch forward eight threads then bring the needle back four threads (fig 2).

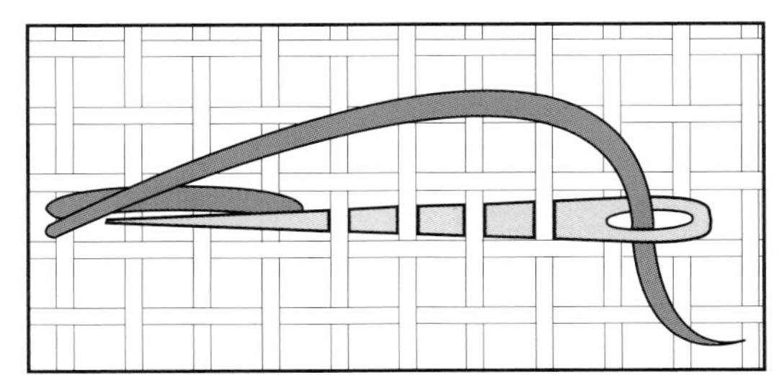

fig 2

3. Take a second stitch over the last four threads (fig 3). Repeat steps 2 and 3 for the length required.

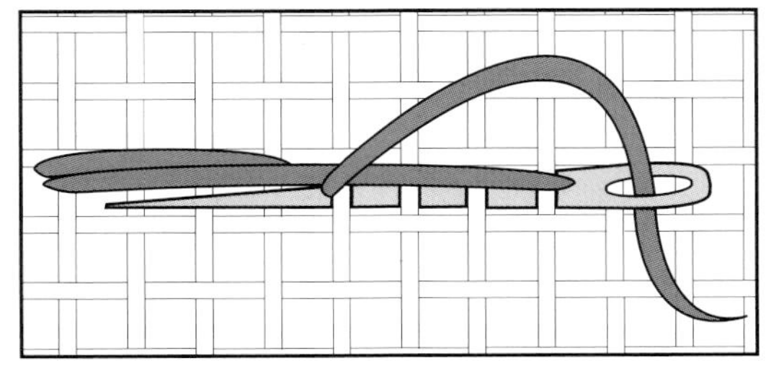

fig 3

To Turn a Corner

When you have worked up to the corner, work the second stitch, which is at the corner, over four threads (step 3). Then take the needle up four threads from the end stitch and bring the needle back out at the corner (fig 4). This will give you a diagonal stitch on the surface of the material but as this is the wrong side of the material it will be hidden in the next row of stitching. Work one stitch over the four threads, now continue steps 2 and 3 until the next corner.

When you have completed the stem stitch, turn your work to the right side and fold the fabric along the line of stem stitches with the stitches creating little 'picots' on the edge of the fold.

fig 4

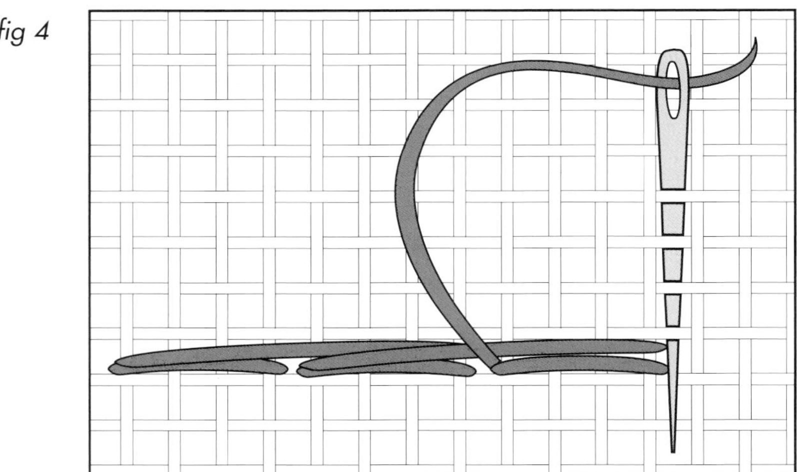

Stage I I - *Edging Stitch - work on the right side of the fabric*
This is worked on the *right* side of the fabric over four threads each way. With a new thread bring your needle out four threads beneath the 'picots' and work two horizontal stitches over the same four threads (fig 5). It is important the stitches are worked directly beneath the 'picots'.

fig 5

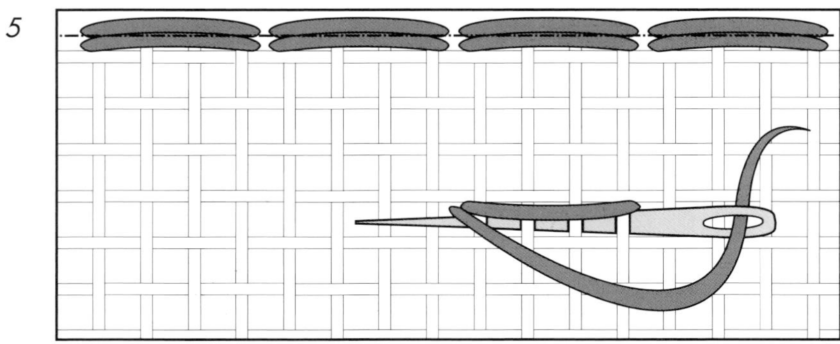

fig 6

Next work two vertical stitches. When you work the second one take your needle four threads along ready to work the next two horizontal stitches (fig 6). Continue in this way until you come to the corner.

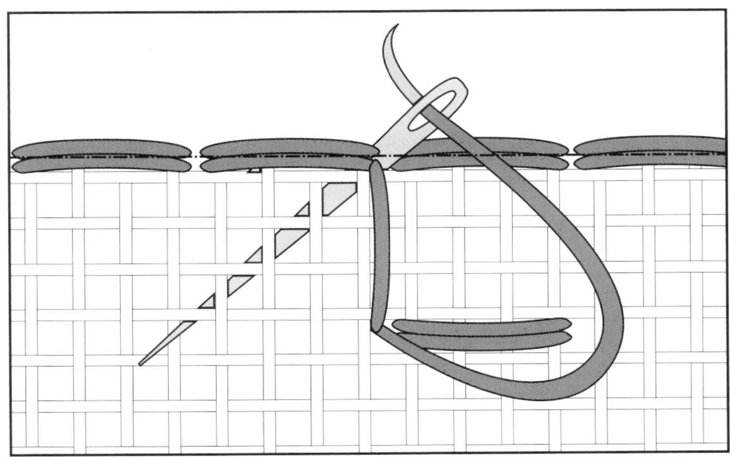

Trim fabric back, after the edging stitch has been worked, to one thread below the stitching. Only trim 5-7cms (2-3") at a time. As a guide for cutting pull out one thread to create a channel to cut along (fig 7).

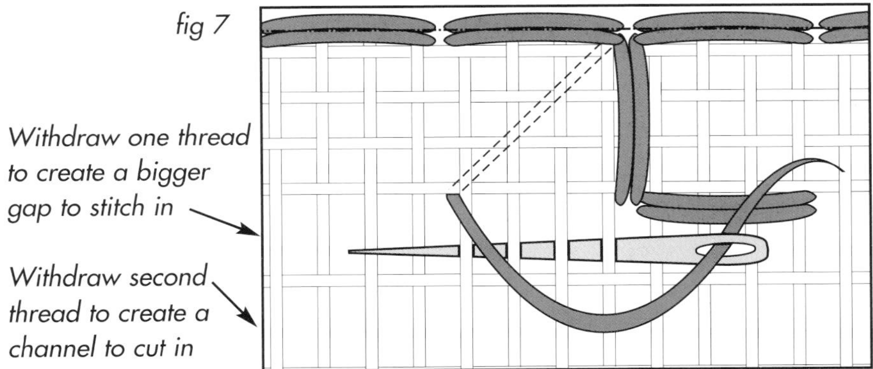
Withdraw one thread to create a bigger gap to stitch in
Withdraw second thread to create a channel to cut in
fig 7

To work round the corner

Two stitches from the corner work the two horizontal stitches - the first part of the next stitch. Stop. Trim the excess fabric away to the outer edge of the fabric (use the withdrawn thread as a cutting guide). Fold back the fabric along the stem stitched line - it will create a nice sharp point - and work three vertical stitches through all the layers of fabric. Now work three more stitches on the other side of the corner (fig 8). Continue stitching in the usual manner.

fig 8

three stitches

HANDY HINT

To make it easier to work the edging stitch, withdraw a thread. For example if the edging stitch is being worked over four threads withdraw the fifth thread down creating a bigger 'gap' for the needle to slip into. This ensures all the stitches are placed correctly. Withdraw the seventh thread to give a cutting line.

How to Stitch a Perfect Mitred Corner Every Time

To stitch a perfect mitred corner the time spent in preparation is essential. Decide where your hem is to fold into. This is the inside edge of the hem and the first line of tacking must go here - the solid line in the diagram (fig1).

fig 1

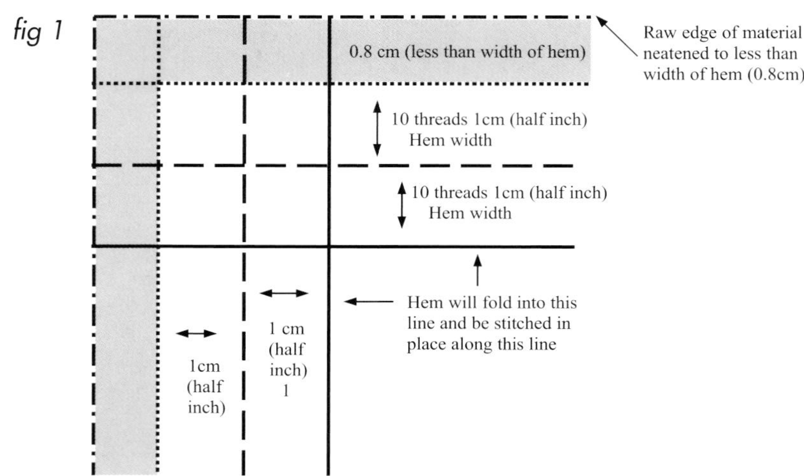

Decide on the width of the hem. Ours is 10 threads wide so all lines are tacked 10 threads apart. (You may prefer to measure a distance rather than count threads - the equivalent distance would be1cm or half an inch.)

Tack a second line - the long dashed line - 10 threads from the inner line of tacking.

Tack a third line - the dotted line - 10 threads from the second line of tacking.

fig 2

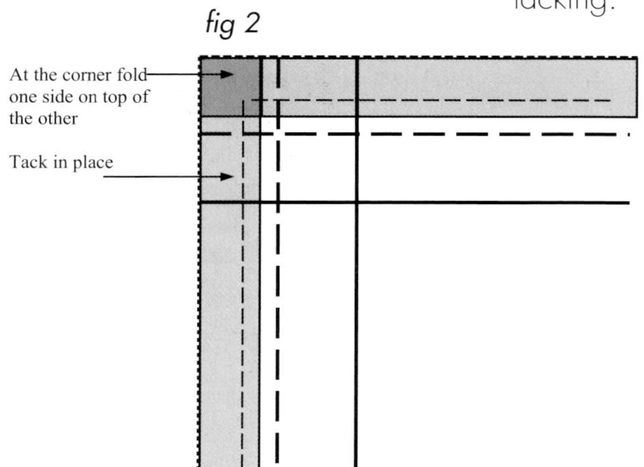

Trim your fabric back so that the material extending beyond the third line of tacking is slightly less than the width of the hem (fig 1).

Fold the shaded area in, at the corners fold one side on top of the other and tack in place (fig 2).

Now fold each corner down to the inner tacked corner, tack across the diagonal to hold fabric in place and cut the shaded area off (fig 3).

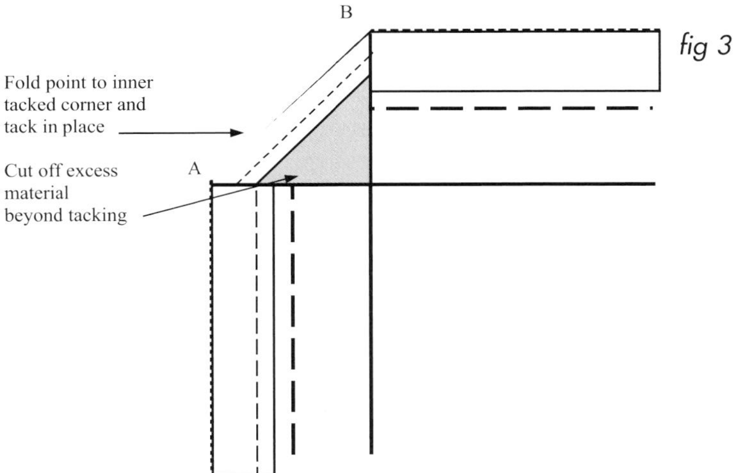
B
Fold point to inner tacked corner and tack in place
A
Cut off excess material beyond tacking

fig 3

Pick up the fabric and fold the corner between the finger and thumb, pinching it together tightly so that points 'A' and 'B' are together. Using fine thread over sew the corner together, starting where indicated. At the edge put your finger inside to ensure the fabric is spread flat and then lay the mitred corner against the inner line of tacking and work two or three stitches at the corner to hold it exactly in position. Stitch all four mitred corners before hemming the sides.

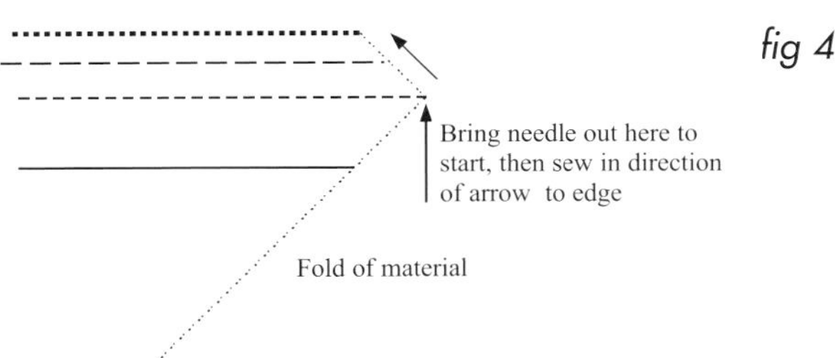
Bring needle out here to start, then sew in direction of arrow to edge
Fold of material

fig 4

HANDY HINT

When pressing your work put a folded tablecloth on the table and lay your embroidery face down on the tablecloth before pressing. The tablecloth has a little 'give' which prevents your embroidery being completely flattened! If you do by chance 'flatten' your embroidery with over enthusiastic ironing rinse again in clean water and then iron gently.

Queen Stitch *(also known as Rococo stitch)*

This pretty, diamond shaped stitch is found on samplers from the seventeenth century onwards. It is four threads high with all stitches sharing the same space at both the top and bottom. Each stitch is anchored in the centre over a different thread. It is usually worked with a little tension on the vertical stitches. While not quick to stitch it does give a most attractive end result. It is worked from right to left. If you have difficulty practise on a piece of canvas or 18 count linen.

fig 1

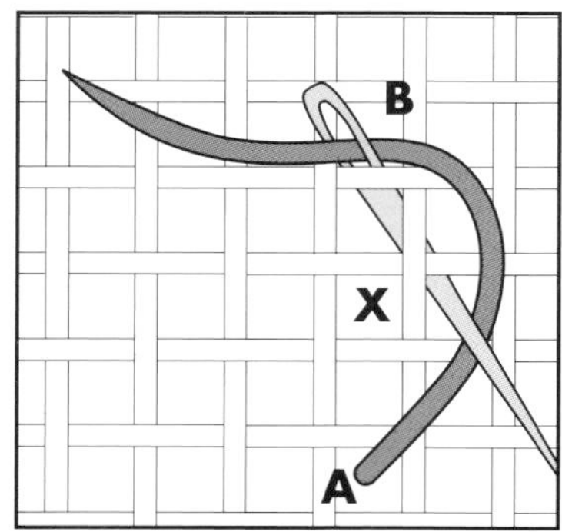

x = centre

1. To start bring the thread to the front at the base of the diamond (A) count up four threads and take the needle down (B) bringing it back to the front two threads down and one thread to the right of the centre (fig 1). Pull the stitch a little to create small holes at the top and bottom.

fig 2

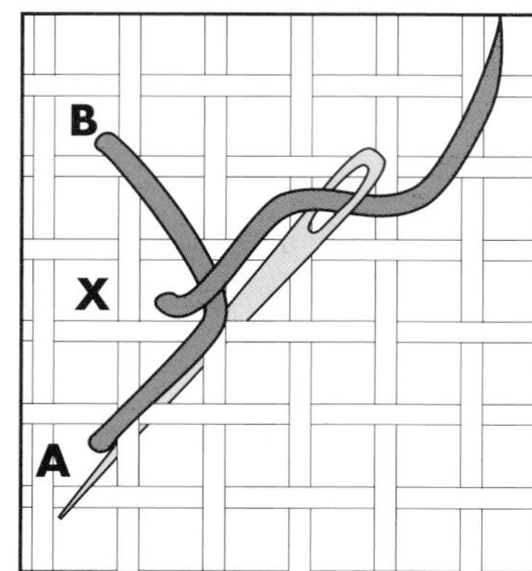

2. Anchor this thread in position by stitching over one vertical thread (the vertical thread is the second thread out from the centre) bring your needle back out at the base of the diamond (A) ready for the next stitch (fig 2).

fig 3

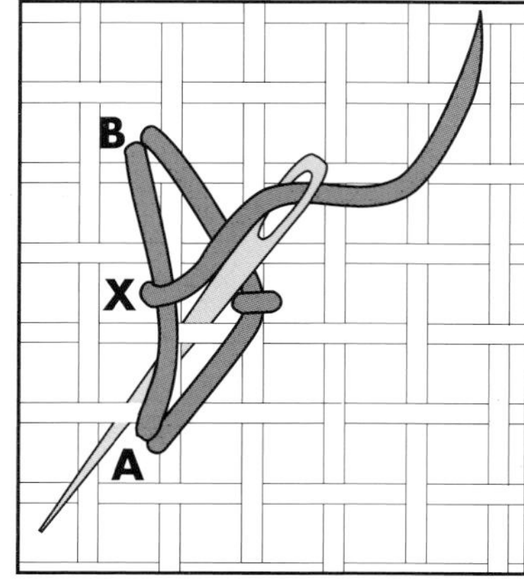

3. Take a second stitch from (A) to (B) but bring the needle out in the centre and anchor this thread by stitching over the vertical thread just to the right of the centre (fig 3).

4. Take a third stitch from (A) to (B) bringing the needle out one thread to the left of the centre (fig 4), hold the loop of thread to the left and then insert the needle into the fabric as shown (fig 5). With the needle in position pull the thread taut before pulling the needle through the fabric, thereby anchoring the stitch at the centre. By placing the needle this way the vertical thread is held in place while a little tension is put on the stitch before pulling the needle through the fabric to anchor it at the centre. It is also easier to see that you are placing your needle correctly with the loop of thread held to the left.

5. Repeat for the fourth stitch (fig 6).

This stitch is often worked in blocks but in the Adam and Eve Sampler it is worked as individual diamonds spaced around the text.

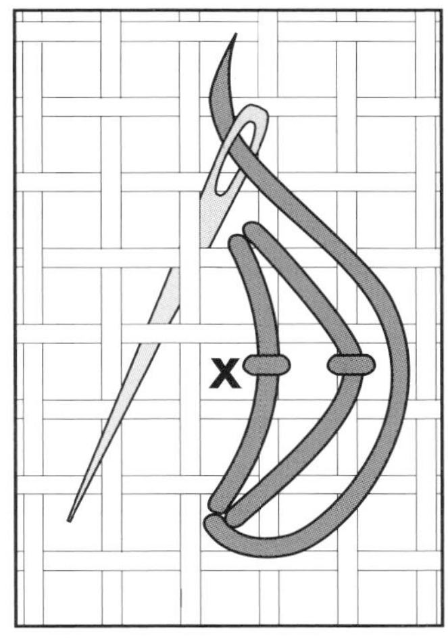

fig 4

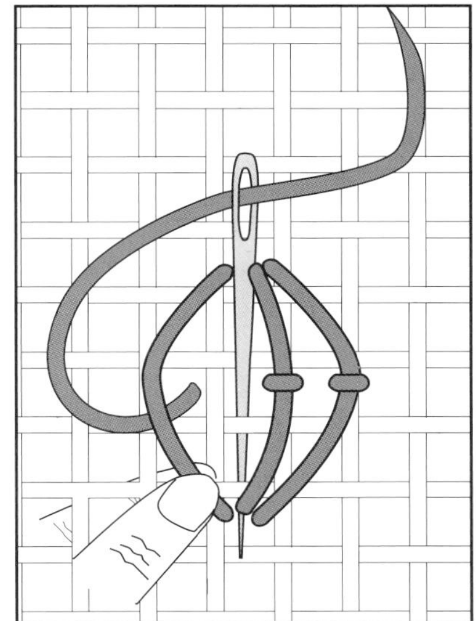

fig 5

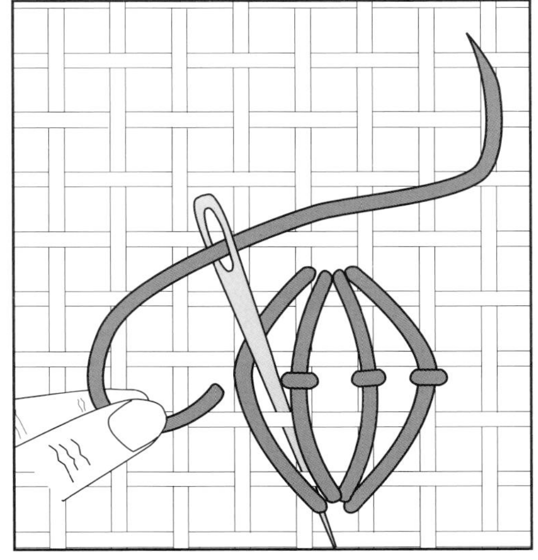

fig 6

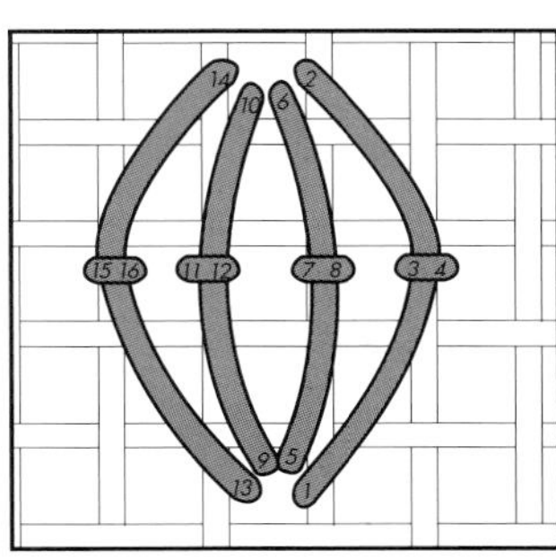

fig 7 Completed stitch

Adam & Eve

Whatsoever thy had findeth to do,
Do it with thy might.

Ecclesiastes 9-10

This sampler is named for the Adam and Eve motif that appears on it and continues the strong tradition of using Biblical motifs on samplers. Historically books were precious, very expensive and the only book in most households was a Bible. Knowledge of its contents was very thorough and people were steeped in its imagery. These biblical motifs created a strong tradition of pictorial imagery in samplers.

The very earliest English samplers still in existence do not include human figures. The earliest dated example of an English sampler with figures is a Random Sampler of 1630 which shows figures which are possibly the parents of the worker, holding hands[1]. From this period onwards figures are well represented on all types of samplers including the cut, drawn and lacework variety.

There are a number of biblical motifs that have appeared on samplers including, Elijjah in the Wilderness, The Spies of Canaan, The Five Wise and Five Foolish Virgins, Faith, Hope and Charity among others, plus symbols that represent different aspects of Christian beliefs. Possibly the best known motif, and the earliest of the biblical motifs featuring human figures, is the Adam and Eve motif. This has appeared on samplers since the eighteenth century, becoming quite common in the latter half of that century. The two figures appear clothed or naked and a typical verse which appears beneath them is

Adam and Eve whilst innocent

In paradise were placed

But soon the serpent by his wiles

The happy pair disgraced[2]

Coming from a family with strong Christian beliefs which I have always enjoyed living within, I wanted to stitch an 'Adam and Eve' sampler using strong colours to give it vibrancy.

[1] *Samplers Five Centuries of a Gentle Craft, Anne Sebba, Weidenfeld and Nicolson, London, 1979, P 37.*
[2] *Traditional Samplers, Sarah Don, Macmillan, Australia, 1986, P 18.*

Linen

The Adam and Eve Sampler is stitched on natural linen with 35 threads to the inch using one thread of stranded cotton. These instructions are for stitching the sampler using linen with 28 - 35 threads per inch any of which will produce a most attractive end result. If you wish to use a different linen, refer back to my earlier more detailed notes about the type of linen to buy and select a linen that you will enjoy holding, working with and that will last well in the years ahead. (See page 6.)

This sampler is stitched using cross stitch, Holbein and Queen stitch. The Queen stitch is used in the border around the text and a Holbein stitch alternative is given. The edge is finished with Scandinavian Edging stitch. Alternatively Antique hem stitch could be used. Detailed information on both these options is given on pages 14 and 15.

Starting and finishing neatly is important and a number of different methods for both are recommended, any of which will give a very neat final result see page 9.

Design width 122 x 142 stitches length or 244 x 284 threads.

Allow an additional two threads between the stitching and the edging and allow a further eight threads in total for the edging.

The fabric allowance has been calculated based on finishing this sampler with a Scandinavian Edging Stitch hem. Should you wish to mount or finish this Sampler with an Antique Hem stitched edge allow extra fabric.

Linen

Threads per inch	*Finished Size*	*Quantity to Purchase*
35	18 x 21cm 7 x 8 1/4in	25cm sq. 10in sq.
31	19.5 x 23cm 7 3/4 x 9in	25 x 30cm 10 x 12in
30	20.5 x 24cm 8 x 9 1/2in	25 x 30cm 10 x 12in
28	22 x 25.5cm 9 x 10 1/2in	28 x 35cm 11 x 14in

Threads Adam and Eve Sampler

This sampler was stitched using one thread of stranded cotton throughout. For more information on threads to use see page 6.

DMC	Anchor	Au Ver a Soie - D'Alger
347	1025	2924
471	265	2114
725	297	2514 Snake's eye only
829	906	526
839	1050	3433
936	269	2136
937	268	516
950	4146	2912
995	410	114
3328	1024	2915
3346	267	2115
3347	266	244
3362	862	3726
3750	1036	1716/1715
3765	169	126

The secret of happiness is not doing what one likes, but in liking what one has to do.

James M Barrie

Starting the Design

Neaten the raw edges of the linen by hand or machine. (See Before you Begin, page 9.)

Tack the centre of the sampler horizontally and vertically over four threads. My preference is to work the border round the outside of the sampler first, then work from the top down starting at the centre and working out to the edge in each direction.

Alternatively you could start at the centre top and work down, stitching the border as you go, as long as you keep the border ahead of the motifs to ensure they all line up correctly.

When charting this design ready for publication I noticed there were a number of minor variations in my stitching. On each page with the section of the chart given I note these variations and additional stitching information. Please read through these notes before you start to stitch and then you may choose to change these or stitch them as I have. Numbers referred to in these notes are for DMC threads.

To Finish

This sampler is completed with Scandinavian edging stitch see page 15 for detailed instructions for this stitch. The first row of stem stitch is worked six threads beyond the cross stitching over four threads using Colour 644 in No 12 Perle on 31 - 35 count linen and No 8 Perle on 28 - 30 count linen. The second row of stitching is worked using sewing thread to match the linen.

Chart pages 26-27

Chart pages 28-29

Chart pages 30-31

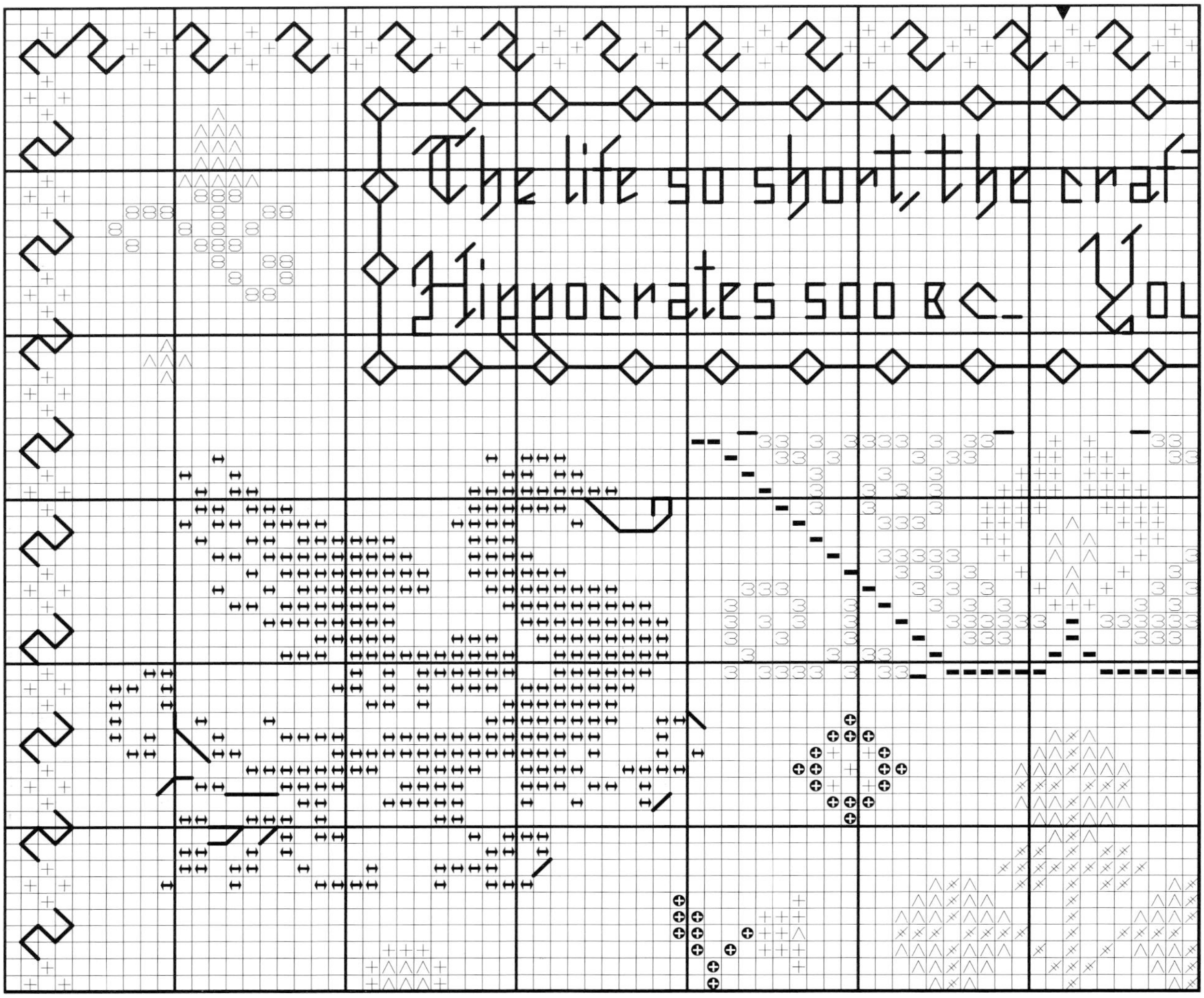

Top third of Adam and Eve Sampler

Refer to the colour photograph page 47 for additional detail

Outer border	The Holbein stitch is worked in green (937) and the cross stitch is worked in red (347).
Text	Stitched using 3362

COLOUR KEY

△	= DMC : 3328	↔	= DMC : 3765	⨯	= DMC : 3347	▬	= DMC : 936	⁘	= DMC : 725
+	= DMC : 347	○	= DMC : 3362	▼	= DMC : 995	3	= DMC : 3346	◇	= DMC : 839
8	= DMC : 471	□	= DMC : 950	⊕	= DMC : 937	9	= DMC : 3750	↓	= DMC : 829

Shaded area indicates overlap from previous page

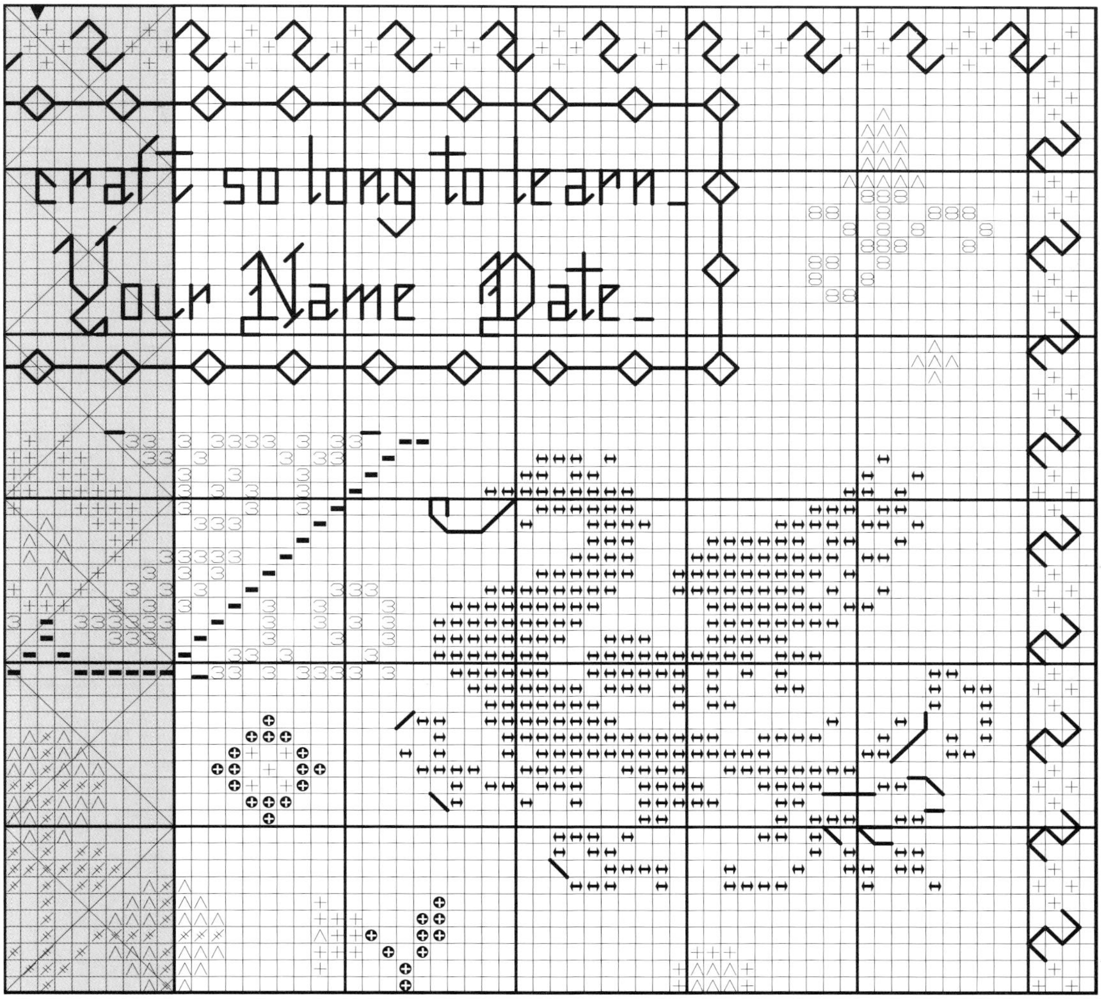

craft so long to learn_

Your Name Date_

Border around text

Stitched using 937

At the vertical left and right hand ends there are 6 threads between the first and second and second and third diamonds, but 8 threads between the third and fourth diamonds.

The diamonds are worked in Queen stitch using the same green thread. The Queen stitch could be replaced with a Holbein stitch outline of the diamond.

Dragon

Placement of dragon in relation to central motif - to left hand side body 6 threads - to right hand side body 4 threads.

Dragon wings are not completely symmetrical.

Tongue is backstitched using 347

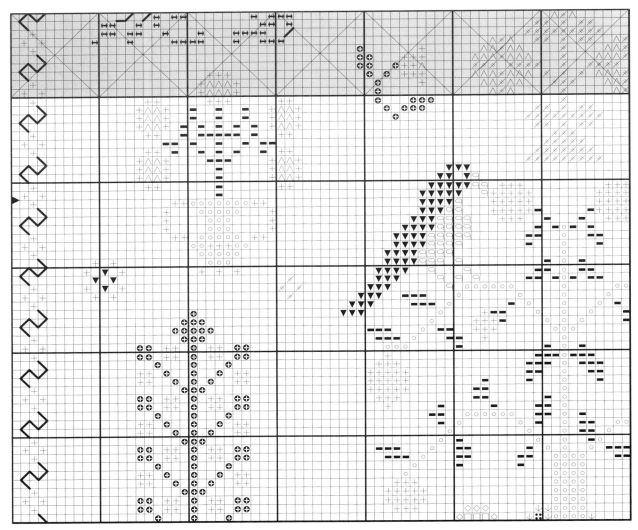

Centre of Adam and Eve Sampler

Shaded areas indicate overlaps from previous page
Refer to the colour photograph page 47 for additional detail

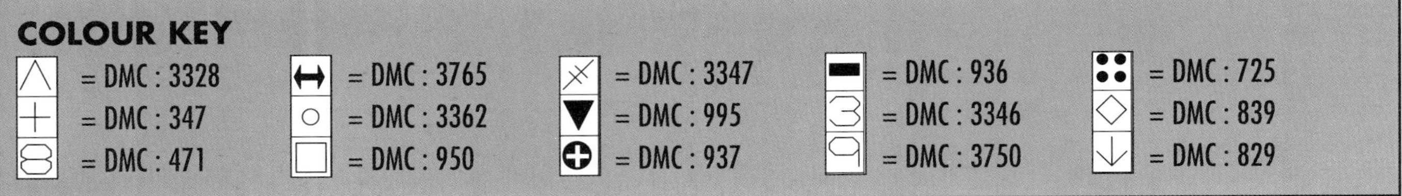

Shaded area indicates overlap from previous page

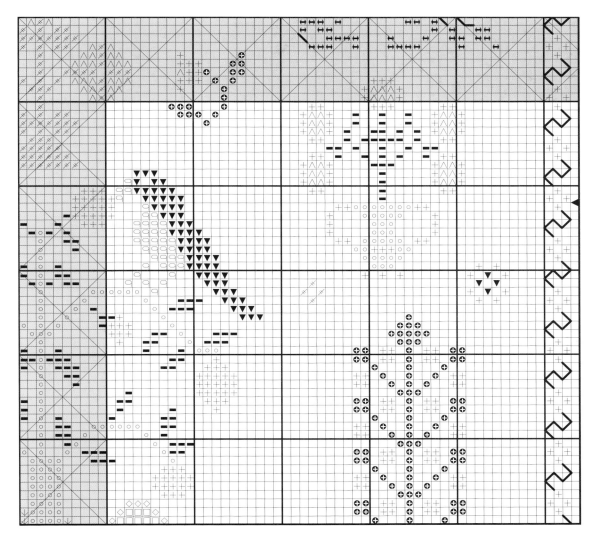

Flowers in pot above side trees

Note irregularity in stitching of stem in right hand side flowers

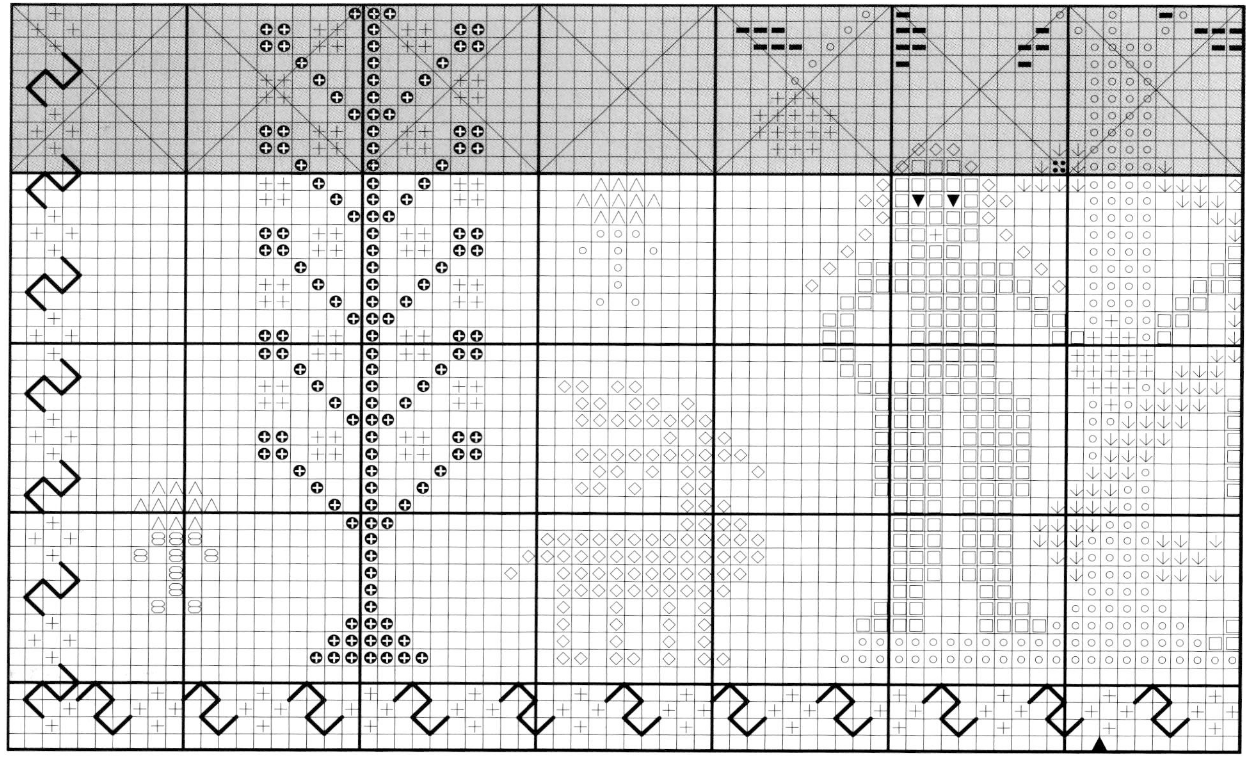

Bottom of Adam and Eve Sampler

Shaded areas indicate overlaps from previous page
Refer to the colour photograph page 47 for additional detail

COLOUR KEY

△	= DMC : 3328	↔	= DMC : 3765	×	= DMC : 3347	▬	= DMC : 936	⁘	= DMC : 725
+	= DMC : 347	○	= DMC : 3362	▼	= DMC : 995	3	= DMC : 3346	◇	= DMC : 839
8	= DMC : 471	□	= DMC : 950	⊕	= DMC : 937	9	= DMC : 3750	↓	= DMC : 829

Shaded area indicates overlap from previous page

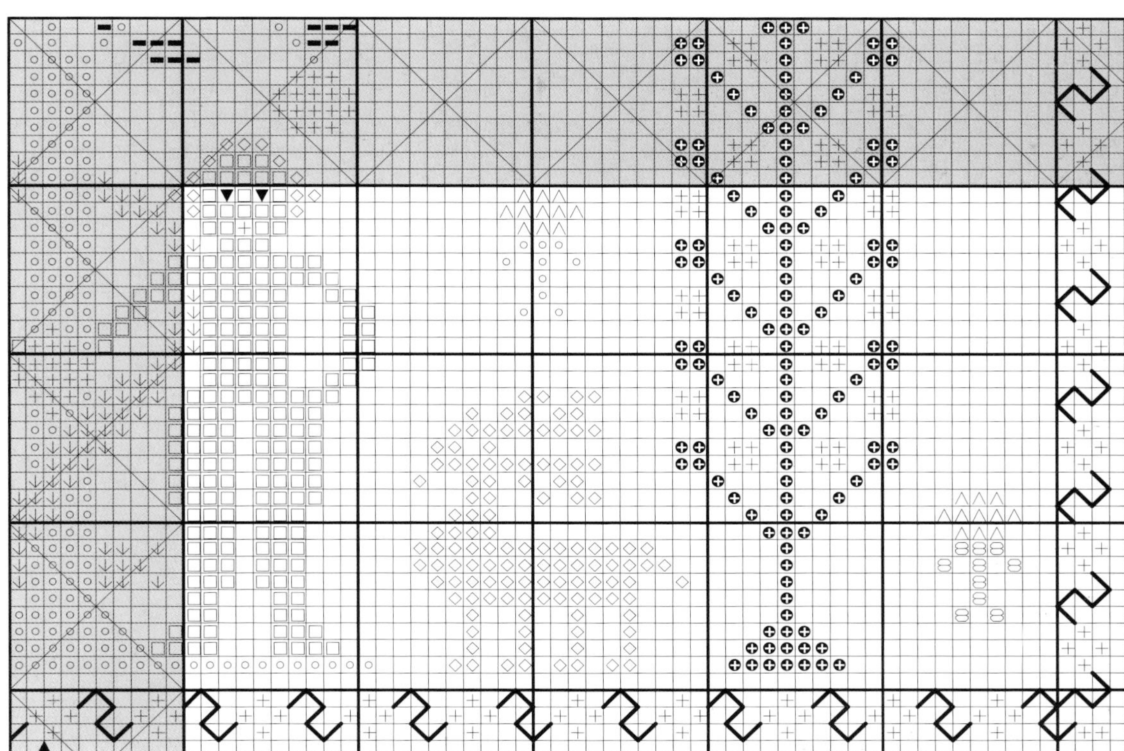

Tree of Life (centre)	All apples even horizontally except lowest two (above Adam and Eve)
Adam and Eve	Notice that Eve ends stands on a double row of cross stitch whereas Adam stands on a single row. Eve is smaller than Adam.
Stags	Left hand stag - Tail does not line up beneath left hand tree, one front leg is missing foot - Body 28 threads horizontally at widest point. Front foot 12 threads from tree of life. Antlers one stitch extends beyond bulk of antlers. Right hand stag - Tail lines up beneath right hand tree, Body 30 threads horizontally at widest point. Front foot 8 threads from tree of life
Side trees	Left tree - 20 threads from border Right tree - 18 threads from border
Small flowers bottom left and right hand corners	Bottom left hand corner - 6 threads from border Bottom right hand corner - 4 threads from border

Pomegranate Sampler

To err is human to
forgive divine.

Alexander Pope's Essay on Criticism

The pomegranate was a symbol of the cycle of life and death as well as the promise of immortality to the ancient Greeks and Hebrews. It was adapted by the early Christians to represent similar themes in the life of Jesus Christ and the Church. To the Buddhists the pomegranate was one of the three blessed fruits: the citrus representing abundance, the peach representing fertility and the pomegranate representing prosperity.

In Greek mythology Persephone (Proserpina) was the beautiful daughter of Demeter (Greek goddess of agriculture) and Zeus (the supreme God in Greek mythology). One day whilst Persephone was out picking flowers the earth opened up underneath her. Hades caught her and took her to the underworld to be his wife.

Demeter immediately looked for her but she was gone without trace. Demeter became very angry at the gods for letting Persephone be taken away so didn't allow her crops to grow. Because of this Zeus commanded Hades to return Persephone to Demeter. But while Persephone was in the underworld, Hades had tricked her into eating a pomegranate, a fruit that stood for marriage. By eating the seeds, she started a marriage with Hades that could not be ended. Zeus arranged a compromise between Demeter and Hades. Persephone would spend two-thirds of the year with her mother and in this time Demeter caused the earth to spring forth with blossom and fruit. In the remaining third of the year which Persephone spent in the underworld with Hades the earth wilted and died as the earth goddess mourned her annual separation from her daughter.

Ancient Hebrews embroidered the pomegranate on religious garments and the fruit was said to have inspired the design of Solomon's crown. There are many references to the pomegranate in the Old Testament and in the New Testament the pomegranate became the symbol of the Resurrection and the hope of eternal life. The many seeds contained in its tough case also made it a symbol of the unity of the many under one authority (either the Church or a secular monarch) and of chastity.

The pomegranate was used in paintings and tapestries in Europe during the Middle Ages and early Renaissance and in the late nineteenth century as a decorative element and as a symbol representing religious and cultural aspects in painting and literature[1]. The pomegranate is crowned with a pendant coronet and for this reason it was appropriated as a decorative device by French and Austrian monarchs[2]. It also features in Chinese poetry and in the near East its abundance of seeds symbolises fertility.

The quotation on this sampler is a combination of many different quotes,

Pomegranate

Whose many seeds symbolise the countless souls, within the different faiths and their hope of eternal life.

I enjoy stitching samplers on a theme. Over the years I have collected these lovely pomegranate designs and the time was right to create this sampler. The colours are shades of coral and yellow-based greens that tone in with the 'tea-dyed' linen.

Be strong and of a good courage
be not afraid,
neither be thou dismayed
for the Lord thy God is with thee
whithersoever thou goest.

The Book of Joshua 1,9.

[1] *Elizabeth Barret, Poems 1844, Lady Geraldine's Courtship "Some Pomegranate, which, if cut deep down the middle, showed heart within blood-tinctured of veined humanity" (lines 164-166)*

[2] *The Gourmet Atlas: The History Origin and Migration of Foods of the World, Susie Ward, Claire Clifton, Jenny Stacey, Macmillan, USA, 1966.*

Linen

My Sampler is stitched on 'tea-dyed' linen with 35 threads to the inch. These instructions are for stitching the Sampler using linen with 28 – 35 threads per inch, all of which will produce a most attractive result. If you wish to use another linen, refer back to my earlier more detailed notes about the type of linen to buy (page 6) and select a linen that you will enjoy holding and working with and that will last well in the years ahead.

Be you to others kind and true
As you'd have others be to you
And never do or say to men
What'er you would
not take again.

Our golden rule
- 1825

The Sampler is stitched using cross stitch and Holbein stitch, mainly for the text. The edge is finished with Scandinavian edging stitch - if you prefer you could lace the completed sampler over card before mounting and framing or you could hem it with Antique hem stitch. Detailed information on these stitches is given on page 9. Starting and finishing neatly is important and I recommend a number of different methods for starting, any of which will give a very neat final result, see page 9.

Design width 129 x 189 stitches length or 258 x 378 threads.

Allow an additional six threads at the top and eight threads in the other three directions as the space between the stitching and the hem and allow a further eight threads in total for the edging.

The fabric allowance has been worked out based on finishing this sampler with a Scandinavian edging stitch, should you wish to mount or finish this sampler with a hem stitched edge allow extra fabric.

Linen		
Threads per inch	*Finished Size*	*Quantity to Purchase*
35	19.5 x 28cm 7 3/4 x 11in	25 x 35cm 10 x 14in
32	21 x 31cm 8 1/2 x 12 1/4in	30 x 40cm 12 x 16in
30	22 x 33cm 9 x 13in	30 x 40cm 12 x 16in
28	24 x 35cm 10 x 14in	35 x 45cm 14 x 18in

Threads Pomegranate Sampler

This sampler was stitched using one thread of stranded cotton throughout. For more information on threads see page 6.

DMC	Anchor	Au Ver a Soie - D'Alger
221	897	4624
347	1025	2924
3773	1008	4612
420	277	525
470	266	244
471	265	2114
730	924	3724
732	281	2124
733	280	2212
734	279	2211
815	20	2925
829	889	526
832	907	2235
3328	1024	2916
3712	1023	2914
3772	1007	4611

To Begin

Neaten the raw edges of the linen by hand or machine, see Before you Begin page 9.

Tack the centre of the sampler horizontally and vertically over two threads. Start by stitching Band 1 across the top of the sampler, centre it over the vertical tacked line and start it a minimum of 2.5cm (1") down from the top edge of the material. (If you are not using Scandinavian edging stitch to complete the sampler remember to allow sufficient material for the finish you have chosen.) Continue working the bands down the sampler. At the same time stitch the side borders to ensure that you are keeping the placement of both the central bands and side borders correct.

When charting this design ready for publication I noticed there were a number of minor variations in my stitching. On each page with the section of the chart given I give these variations and additional stitching information. Please read through these notes before you start to stitch and then you may choose to change these or stitch them as I have. Numbers referred to in these notes are for DMC threads

God grant me the serenity to accept The things I cannot change, Courage to change the things I can and wisdom to know the difference.

To Finish

This sampler is completed with Scandinavian edging stitch, see page 15 for detailed instructions for this stitch. The first row of stem stitch is worked over four threads six threads beyond the cross stitching at the top and eight threads beyond the cross stitching on the other three sides using two threads of 347. This gives a delicate and very subtle touch of colour along the edge of the sampler. The second row of stitching is worked using sewing thread to match the linen.

Left Border **Right Border**

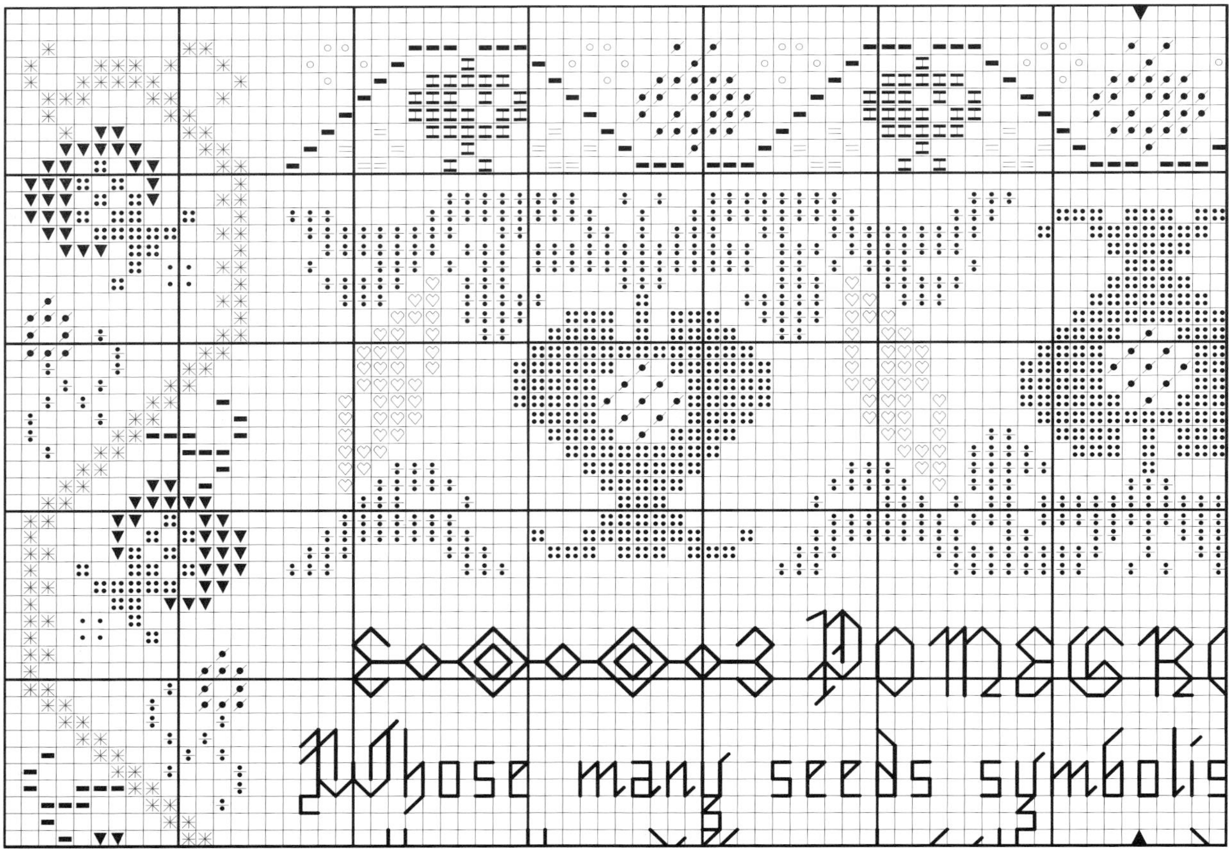

Band 1

Band 2

Band 3 text

Left hand border

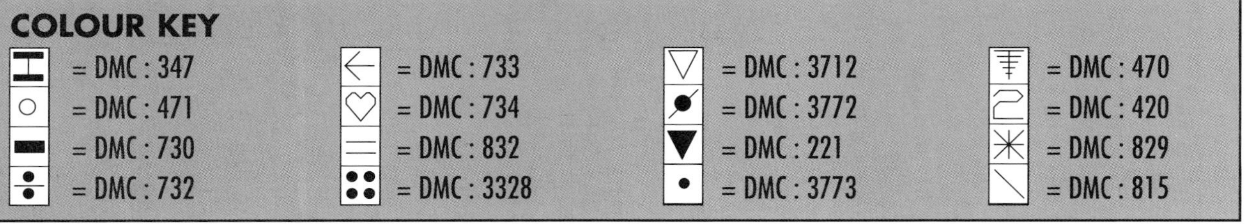

Right hand border

Top Section of Pomegranate Sampler
Band 1 - part of band 3

Refer to the colour photograph page 48 for additional detail
Shaded area indicates overlap from previous page

Band 1 First pomegranate in from left hand side worked in 3772, two of the stitches have not been crossed.

Band 2 The right hand end of the design finishes differently from the start so that there is a two stitch gap at each end.
734 has variations in design
732 not always symmetrical

Band 3 Text 'Pomegranate' stitched using 347. The balance of the text is stitched using 3328. The Holbein stitch motif on either side of the heading is stitched using 732. The left hand motif was stitched one thread to the right, this has been corrected in the chart.
Line of stitching beneath text stroke from lower left to right 3772, from top down 732.

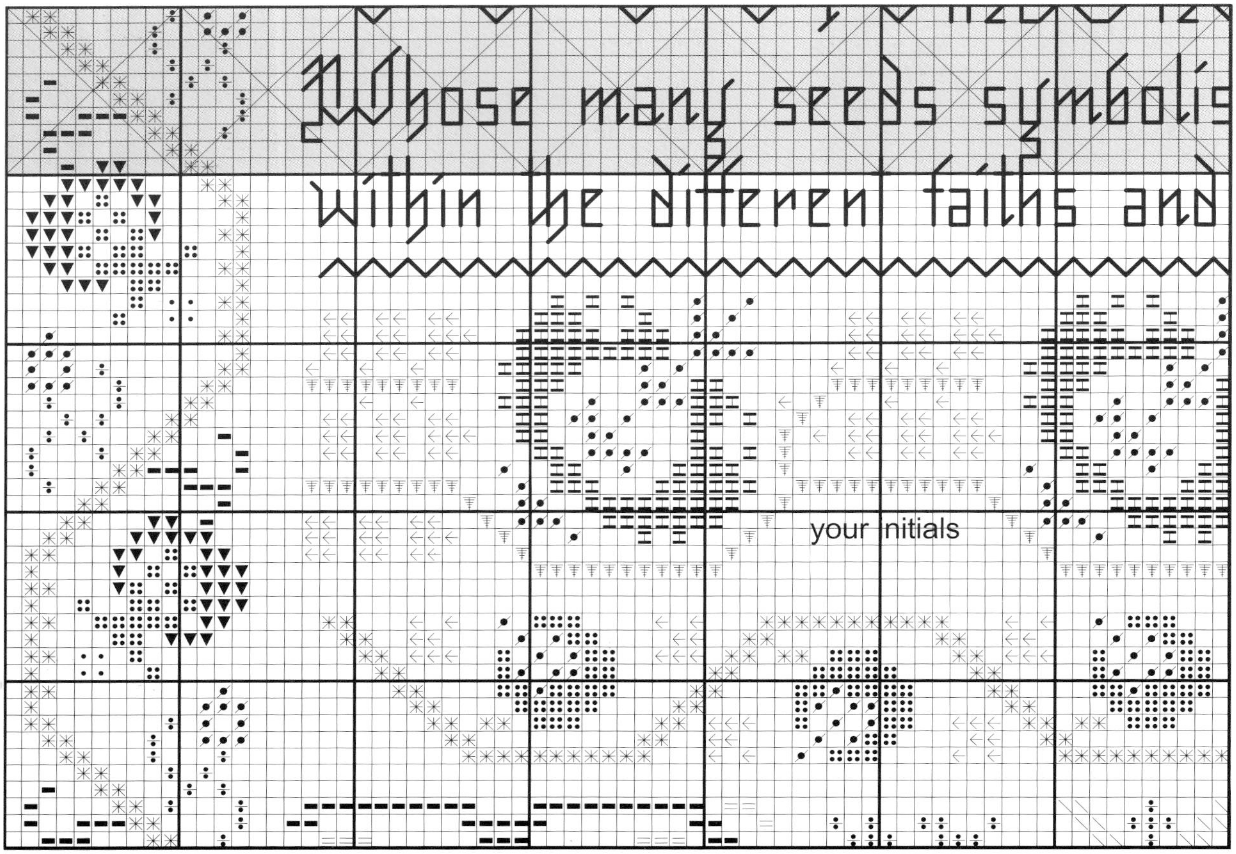

Whose many seeds symbolis

within the different faiths and

your initials

Band 4

Band 5

Left hand border

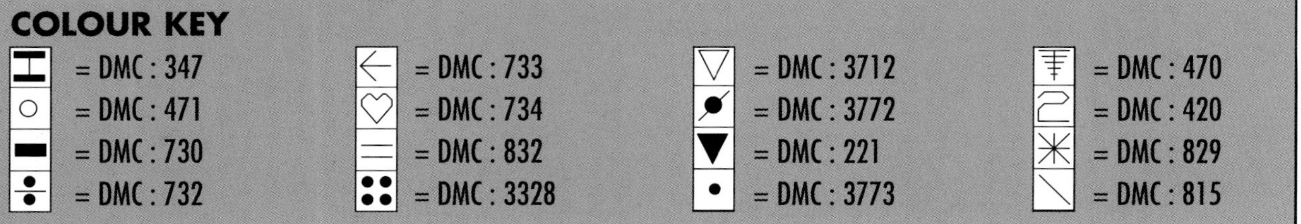

COLOUR KEY

(bar I)	= DMC : 347	←	= DMC : 733	▽	= DMC : 3712	(fir)	= DMC : 470
○	= DMC : 471	♡	= DMC : 734	(dot with line)	= DMC : 3772	(2)	= DMC : 420
▬	= DMC : 730	(double line)	= DMC : 832	▼	= DMC : 221	✳	= DMC : 829
(divide)	= DMC : 732	(four dots)	= DMC : 3328	•	= DMC : 3773	\	= DMC : 815

ouble Band Sampler (DBS)

hown in its entirety

Benedictus benedicat May the Blessed one bless.
1994

Double Band Sampler (DBS)

Top left-hand half

Benedictus benedicat May the Blessed one bless.

Double Band Sampler (DBS)

bottom left-hand half

Double Band Sampler (DBS)

Top right-hand third

Double Band Sampler (DBS)

Middle right-hand third

Double Band Sampler (DBS)

Lower right-hand third

The life so short the craft so long to learn.
Hippocrates 500BC. Olwyn Horwood 1989.

POMEGRANATE
Whose many seeds symbolise the countless souls,
within the different faiths and their hope of eternal life.
OJH
1994

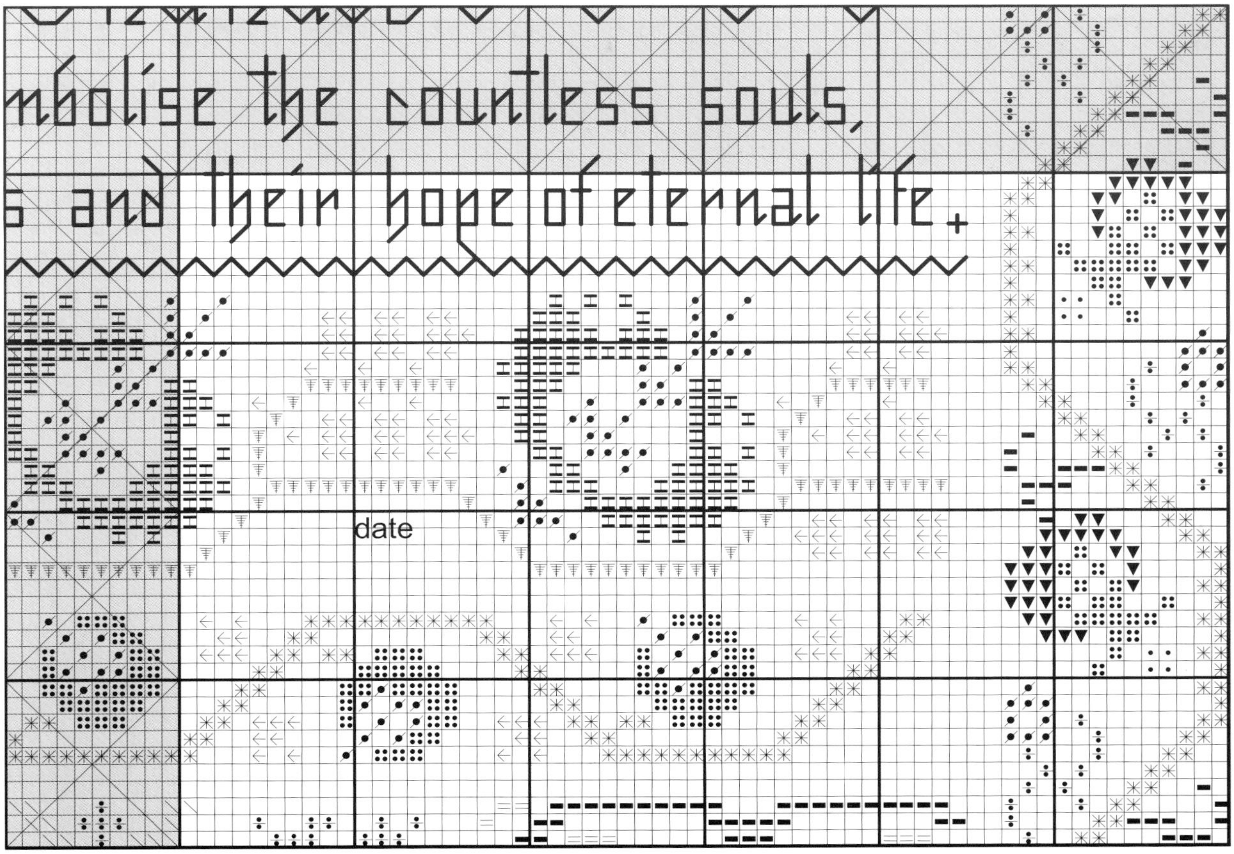

Right hand border

Second Section of Pomegranate Sampler
Rest of band 3 - top of band 6
Shaded areas indicate overlaps from previous page
Refer to the colour photograph page 48 for additional detail

Band 4 Within this band your initials and the date are to be inserted

Band 5 No Variations

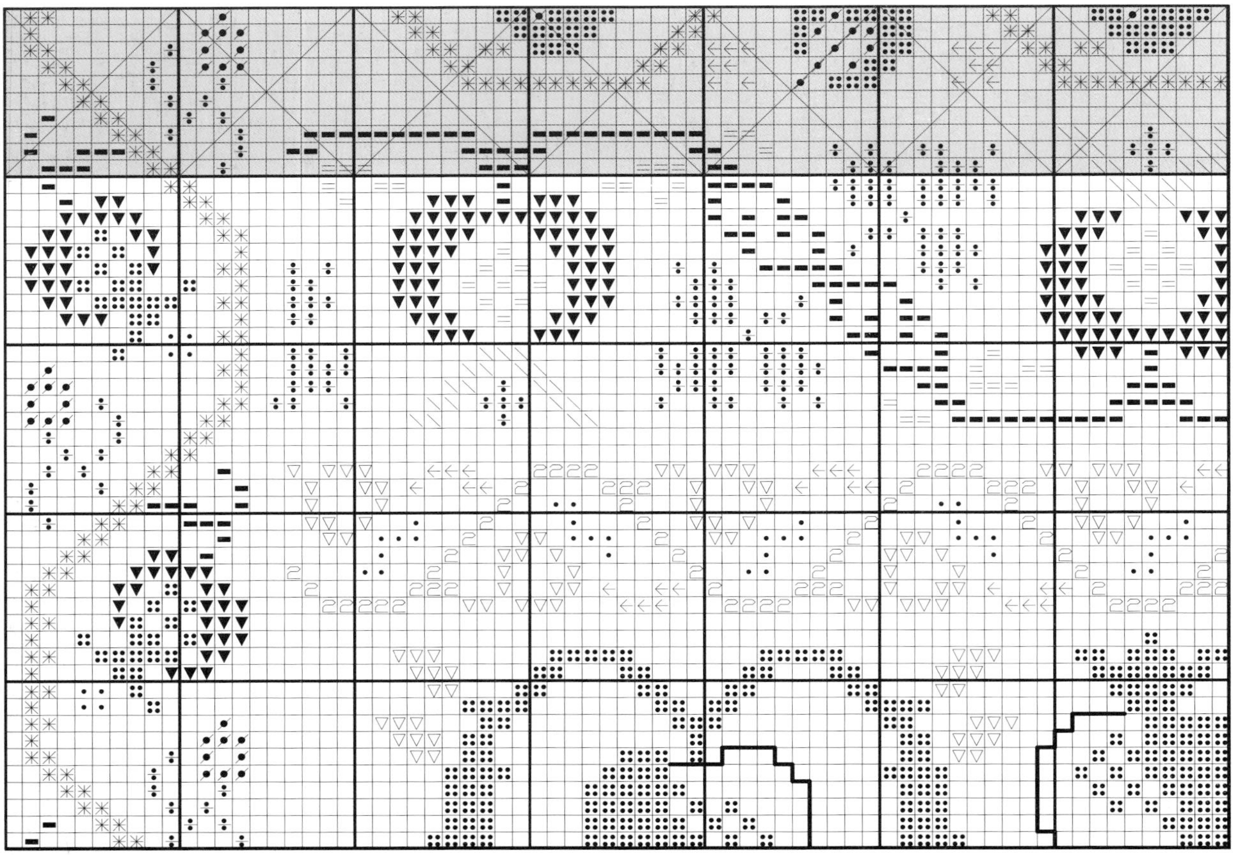

Band 6

Band 7

Band 8

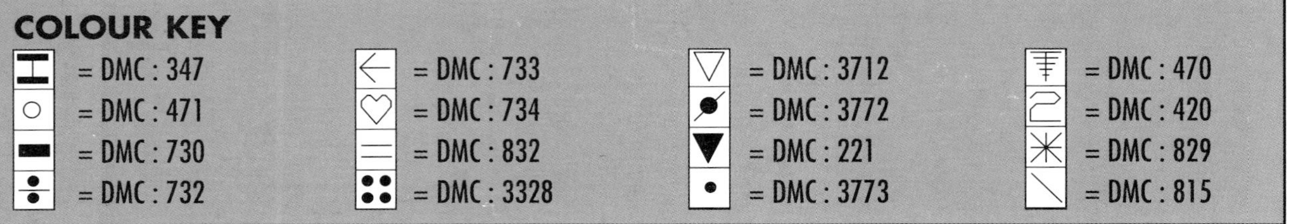

COLOUR KEY

= DMC : 347	= DMC : 733	= DMC : 3712	= DMC : 470
= DMC : 471	= DMC : 734	= DMC : 3772	= DMC : 420
= DMC : 730	= DMC : 832	= DMC : 221	= DMC : 829
= DMC : 732	= DMC : 3328	= DMC : 3773	= DMC : 815

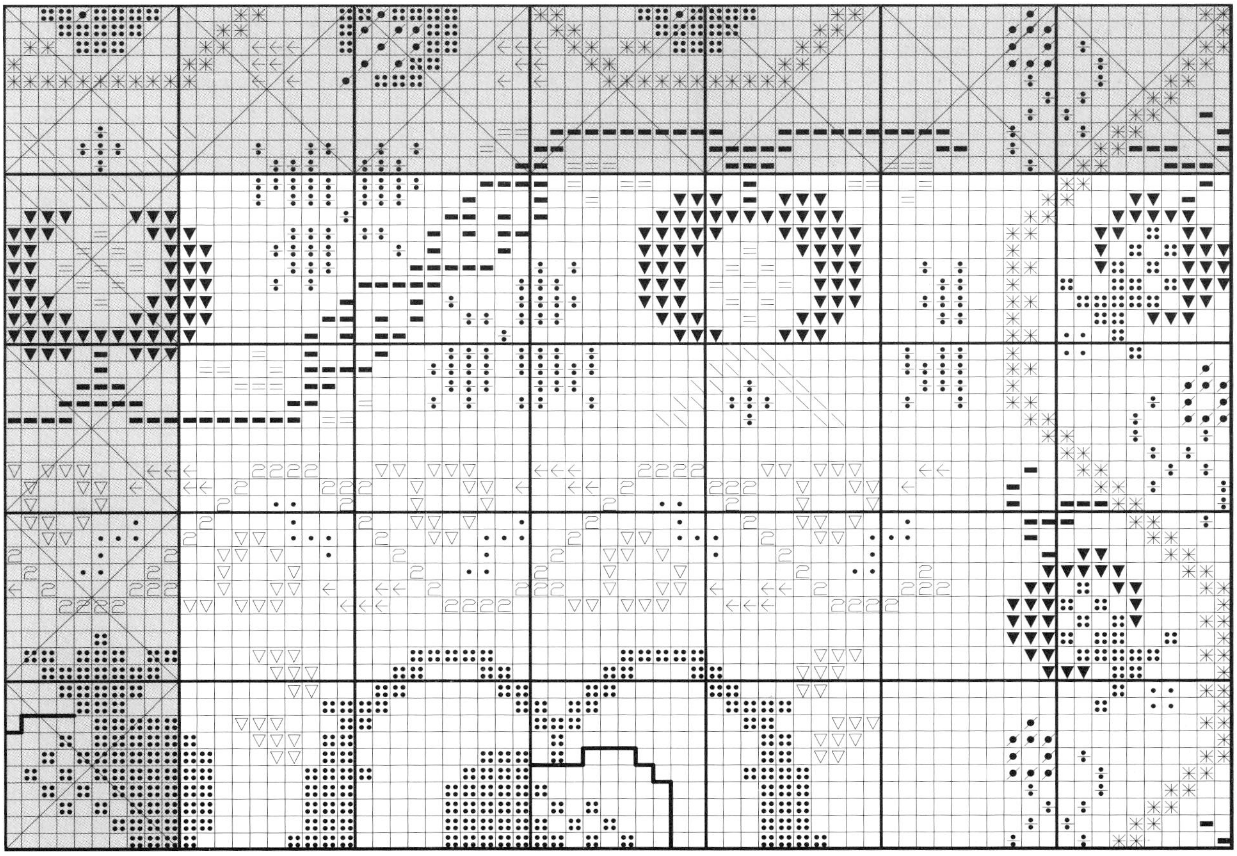

Right hand border

Third Section of Pomegranate Sampler
Rest of band 6 - top half of band 8

Shaded areas indicate overlaps from previous page
Refer to the colour photograph page 48 for additional detail

Band 6 Note difference between 732 at left hand end and right hand end

Band 7 Note extra stitch in straight area at left hand end of main stem

Band 8 I suggest you start stitching this band from the middle pomegranate; position carefully one stitch beneath Band 7

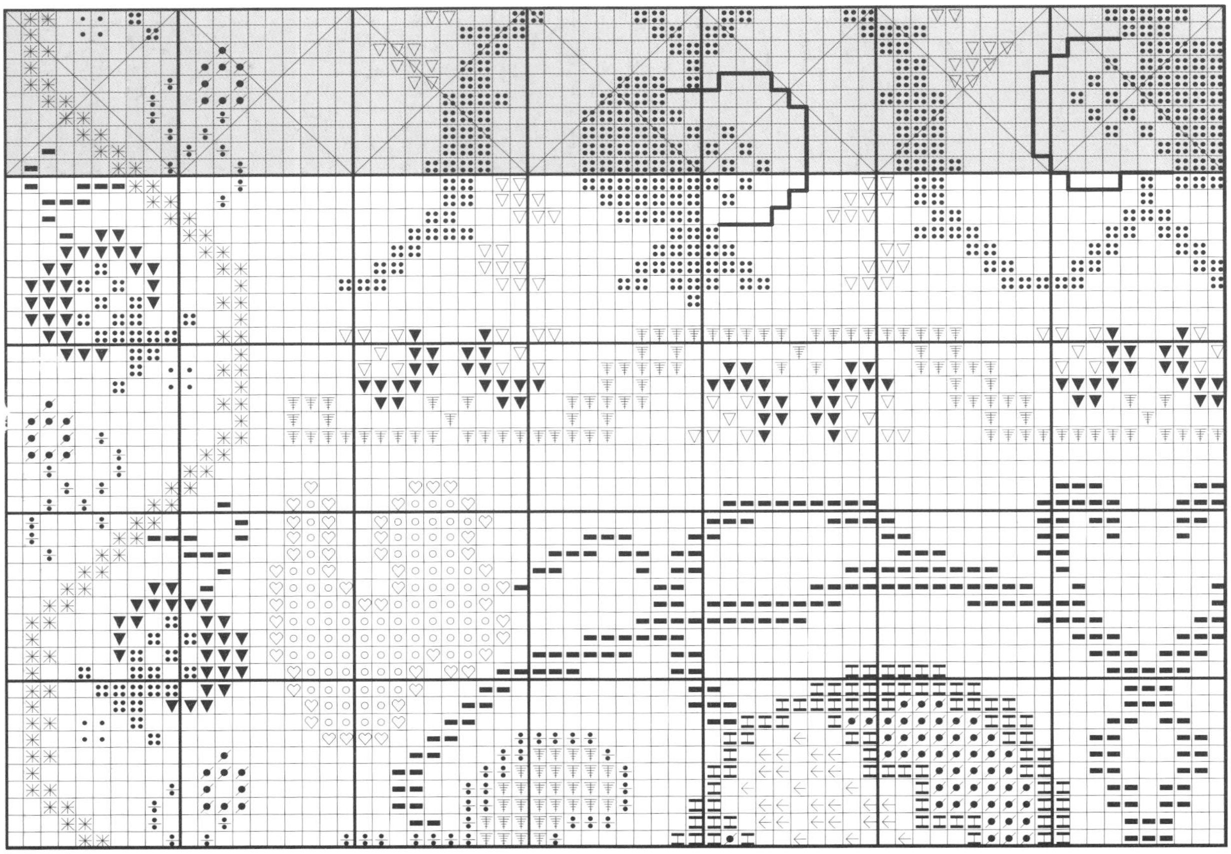

Band 8

Band 9

Band 10

Left hand border

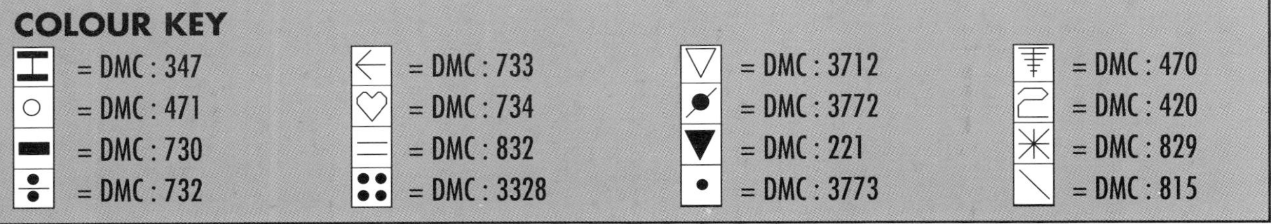

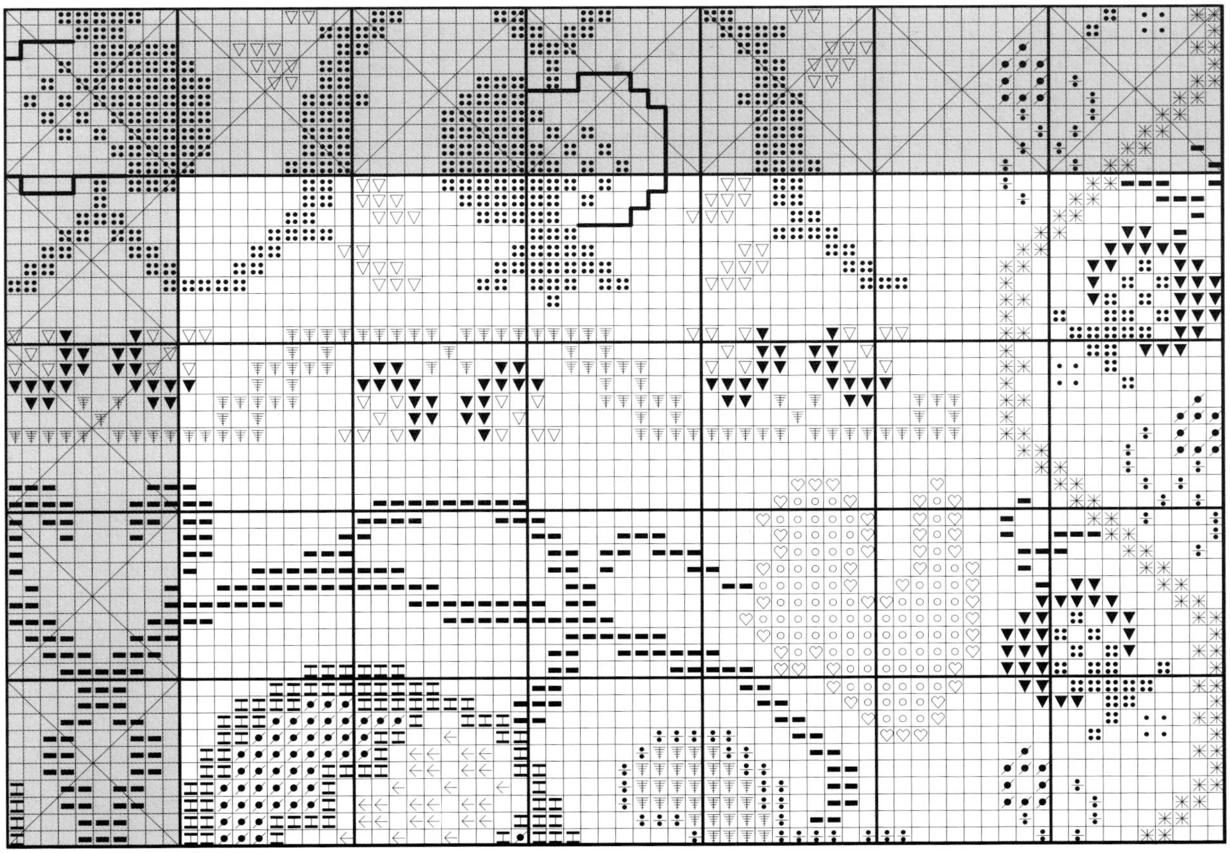

Right hand border

Fourth Section of Pomegranate Sampler
Rest of band 8 - top half of band 10

Shaded areas indicate overlaps from previous page
Refer to the colour photograph page 48 for additional detail

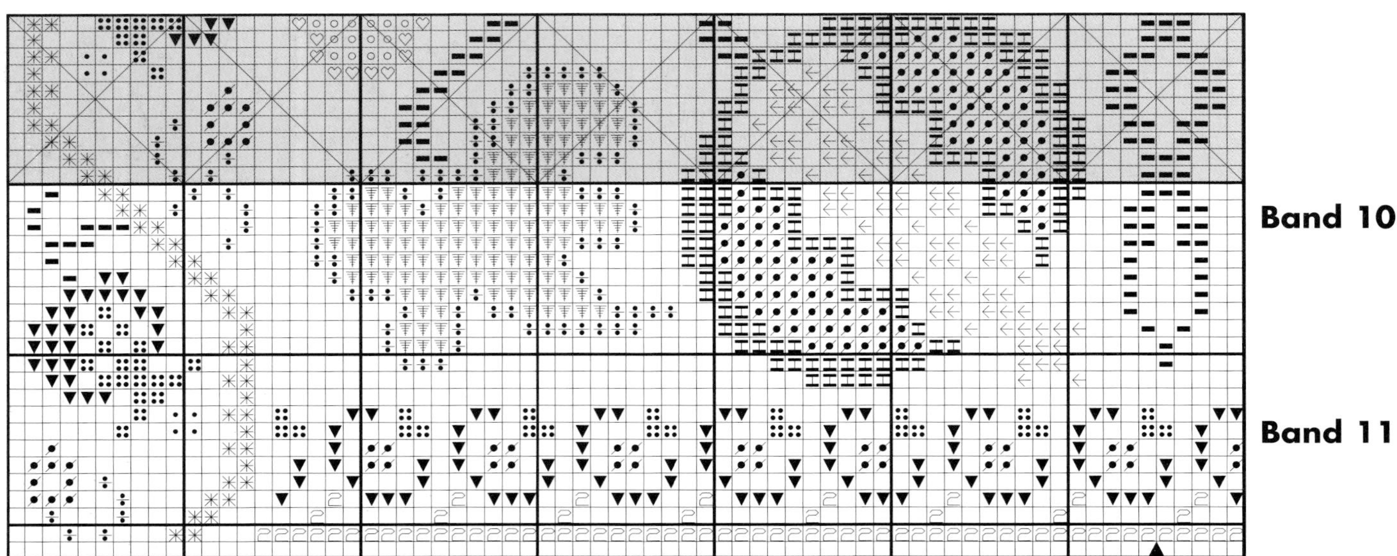

Left hand border

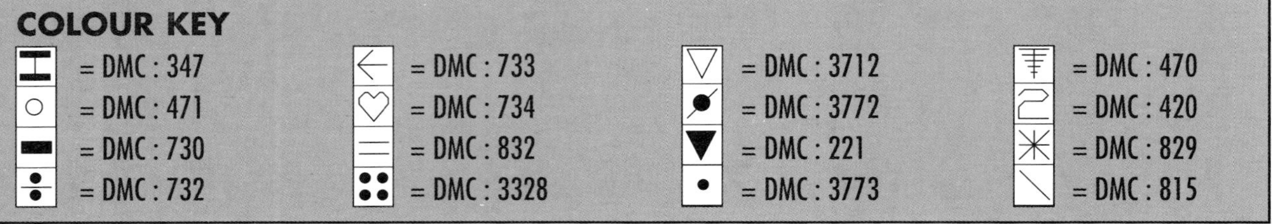

COLOUR KEY

= DMC : 347	= DMC : 733	= DMC : 3712	= DMC : 470
= DMC : 471	= DMC : 734	= DMC : 3772	= DMC : 420
= DMC : 730	= DMC : 832	= DMC : 221	= DMC : 829
= DMC : 732	= DMC : 3328	= DMC : 3773	= DMC : 815

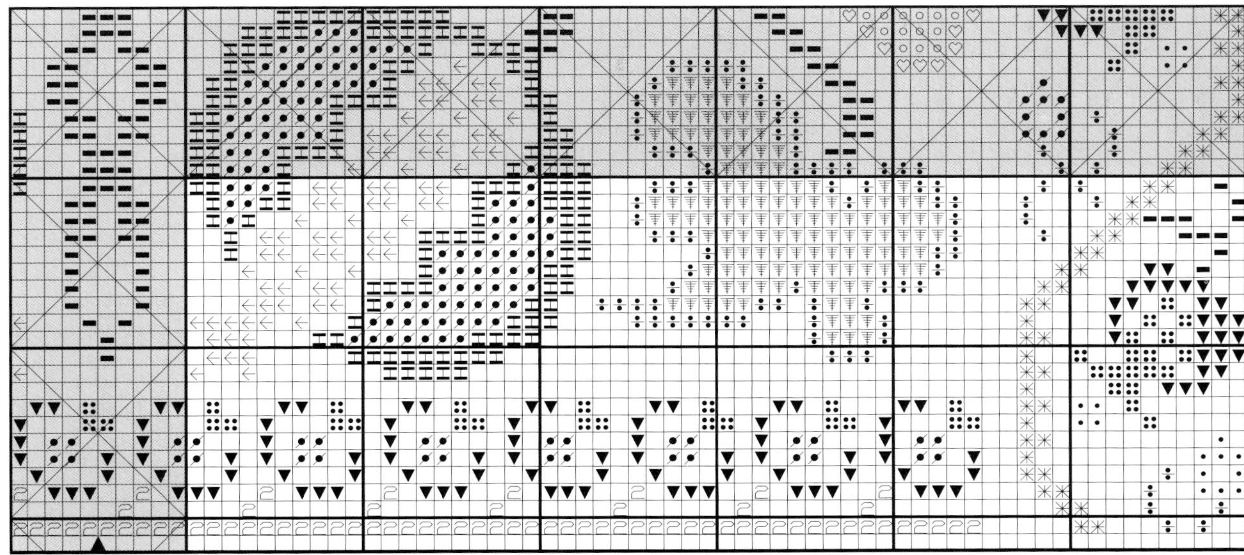

Right hand border

Fifth Section of Pomegranate Sampler
Rest of band 10 and band 11

Shaded areas indicate overlaps from previous page

Refer to the colour photograph page 48 for additional detail

Band 9	No variations
Band 10	Left pale leaf has four cross stitches on base - right hand has three.
Band 11	No variations
Left and right borders	No variations

The Double Band Sampler

Every Old Is New Again

My interest in samplers encouraged me to look twice at a 'double band' sampler which I first saw in an early copy of *Historical Designs for Embroidery*[1] by Louisa Pesel. The sampler is in the Fitzwilliam Museum collection and I subsequently saw a coloured photo of it in the Fitzwilliam Museum Handbook *Samplers*[2].

There are but two lasting
Bequests we can give
our children
The first is roots
The second is wings

The 'double band' layout is not common. Only two samplers with this arrangement of bands and alphabets are known to exist and it is thought that both were stitched as a school room exercise towards the end of the seventeenth century. The second one is kept at Montacute House, Somerset, and dated 1682. Little else is known about them though on the reverse of the sampler held at Montecute House there is an inscription in black silk over ink along the lower edge which reads '*When this was made shee was 11 years olde.*'

The size of this sampler was determined by the bands I visualized using. When travelling some years ago in Austria I bought two books[3] which featured many different deep bands of beasts, people and flowers. These had originally been used as central decorative bands on table linen and on other household furnishings. Elements of these would, I felt, blend together to make a dramatic double band sampler. The alphabet which runs up the centre of the sampler is from an eighteenth century German pattern book[4].

[1] *Historical Designs for Embroidery, Louisa F. Pesel, Batsford Ltd, London, 1956.*
[2] *Fitzwilliam Museum Handbooks - Samplers, Carol Humphrey, Cambridge University Press, United Kingdom, 1997.*
[3] *Alte Volkskunst Kreuzstich ~Ein Werkbuch, Leopold Stocker, Verlag, Graz-Stuttgard, 1993.*
Kreuzstick Muster Aus Graubunden, Ratischen Museum in Chur, Switzerland
[4] *Hersh, Tandy and Charles, Samplers of the Pennsylvania Germans. Birdsboro, Pennsylvania German Society, PA, 1991.*

REQUIREMENTS

Fabric

I chose a pretty light teal blue called Rue Green (shade 707) in Zweigart Belfast 31 count linen, Confederate Grey (shade 718) Pearl Grey (shade 705) and Smokey Pearl (shade 778) are very similar and could be substituted quite happily. A cream linen could also be used as the thread colours would show up beautifully on this. Instructions are given for stitching this sampler using linen with 28 - 35 threads per inch any of which will produce a most attractive end result.

If you wish to use another linen altogether, refer back to my earlier more detailed notes about the type of linen to buy (page 6) and select a linen that you will enjoy holding and working with and that will last well in the years ahead.

The count of the material allowed me a workable number of stitches per inch to display the designs I wished to stitch. The colour is a change from the usual antique white or natural linens which I tend to use and allowed me to work in a most interesting and attractive colour palette. I have used a range of mauves, pinks, blues and greens

Design width 235 by 389 stitch length 470 x 778 threads.

I finished this sampler with mitred corners and a hem stitched edging. If you wish to mount the embroidery or finish it in a different way, allow for this when purchasing the material.

Linen

Threads per inch	*Finished Size*	*Quantity to Purchase*
35	36 x 56cm 14 x 22in	50 x 70cm 20 x 28in
31	41 x 65.5 cm 16 1/4 x 25 3/4in	60 x 80 cm 24 x 32 in
28	43 x 71cm 17 x 28in	60 x 80cm 24 x 32in

Threads Double Band Sampler

This sampler was stitched using one thread of stranded cotton throughout. For more information on threads, see page 6.

DMC	Anchor	Au Ver a Soie - D'Alger
Blanc	2	Blanc
221	897	4624
223	895	4622
316	1017	4633
347	9046	941
414	235	3442
435	308	2245
451	233	3414
452	232	3413
3347	266	2114
502	876	5023
778	968	4631
924	851	1746
926	850	1744
927	848	1742
930	1035	1715
931	1034	1714
932	1033	1712
935	861	3726
988	243	2115
3041	871	5114
3042	870	5113
3051	269	2126
3052	859	3723
3346	268	2116
3362	263	3725
3363	262	1833
3726	1018	4635
3727	1016	4632
3740	873	5115
3768	779	1745
3802	1019	4636

Faith is to believe what
we do not see,
And the reward of
this faith is to
see what we believe.

St. Augustine

To Begin

Neaten the raw edges of the linen by hand or machine, see Before you Begin page 9.

Tack the centre horizontally and vertically over and under two threads using contrasting thread. Tack the horizontal line near the top of the fabric so that the tacking is in a 't' shape. The high horizontal line of tacking is most useful for checking the placement of the bands when you start.

Begin with the vertical alphabet running up the centre then work the letters and the band patterns at the same time so that each is a check on the other.

When charting this design ready for publication I noticed there were some minor variations in my stitching. On each page with the section of the chart given I give these variations and additional stitching information. Please read through these notes before you start to stitch and then you may choose to change these or stitch them as I have.

No bird soars too high if he soars with his own wings

William Blake 1757 - 1827

Double Band Sampler - Stitching Notes

Many of the designs in this Sampler are asymmetrical, this does make the stitching of these designs more challenging.
Numbers referred to in these notes are for DMC threads.

To Finish

For detailed instructions on working Antique hem stitch see page 14 and page 18 for 'How to Mitre a Corner'. Count six threads from the widest point of the pattern on each side then pull the seventh and eighth threads back to where they intersect at the corners. Darn the thread ends from where they meet at the corners towards the edge of the material neatly weaving the ends into the material. The hem is 10 threads deep and counted from the withdrawn threads out. Finish the hem, with mitred corners and hem stitch. Stitch the hem in place first before working the second row of hem stitch on the other side of the withdrawn threads to create ladder hem stitch.

Left Border **Right Border**

Central Band

Note there are differences in spacing in the stitching of the central line of letters and numbers. This is as it is stitched. Also note the movement of 3041 and 414 when stitching up each side of the central line of numbers and letters. Motifs in central band are stitched in Holbein stitch in light lavender 3042 Bell is asymmetrical. 'M' is missing one stitch

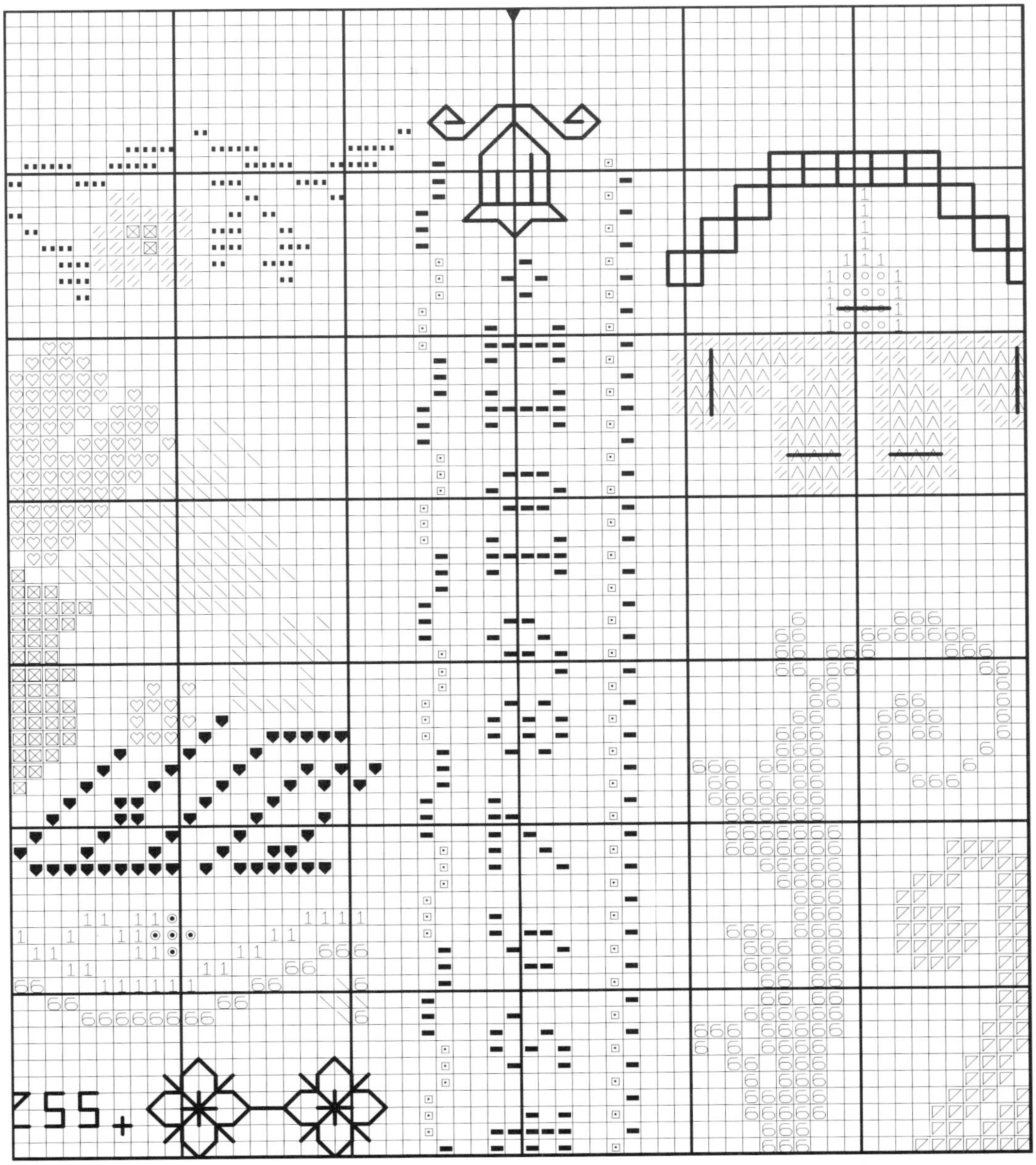

Refer to the colour photograph page 42 for additional detail

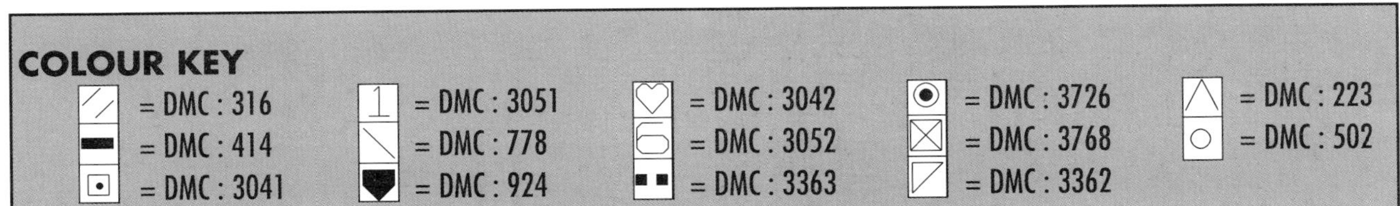

COLOUR KEY
= DMC : 316
= DMC : 414
= DMC : 3041
= DMC : 3051
= DMC : 778
= DMC : 924
= DMC : 3042
= DMC : 3052
= DMC : 3363
= DMC : 3726
= DMC : 3768
= DMC : 3362
= DMC : 223
= DMC : 502

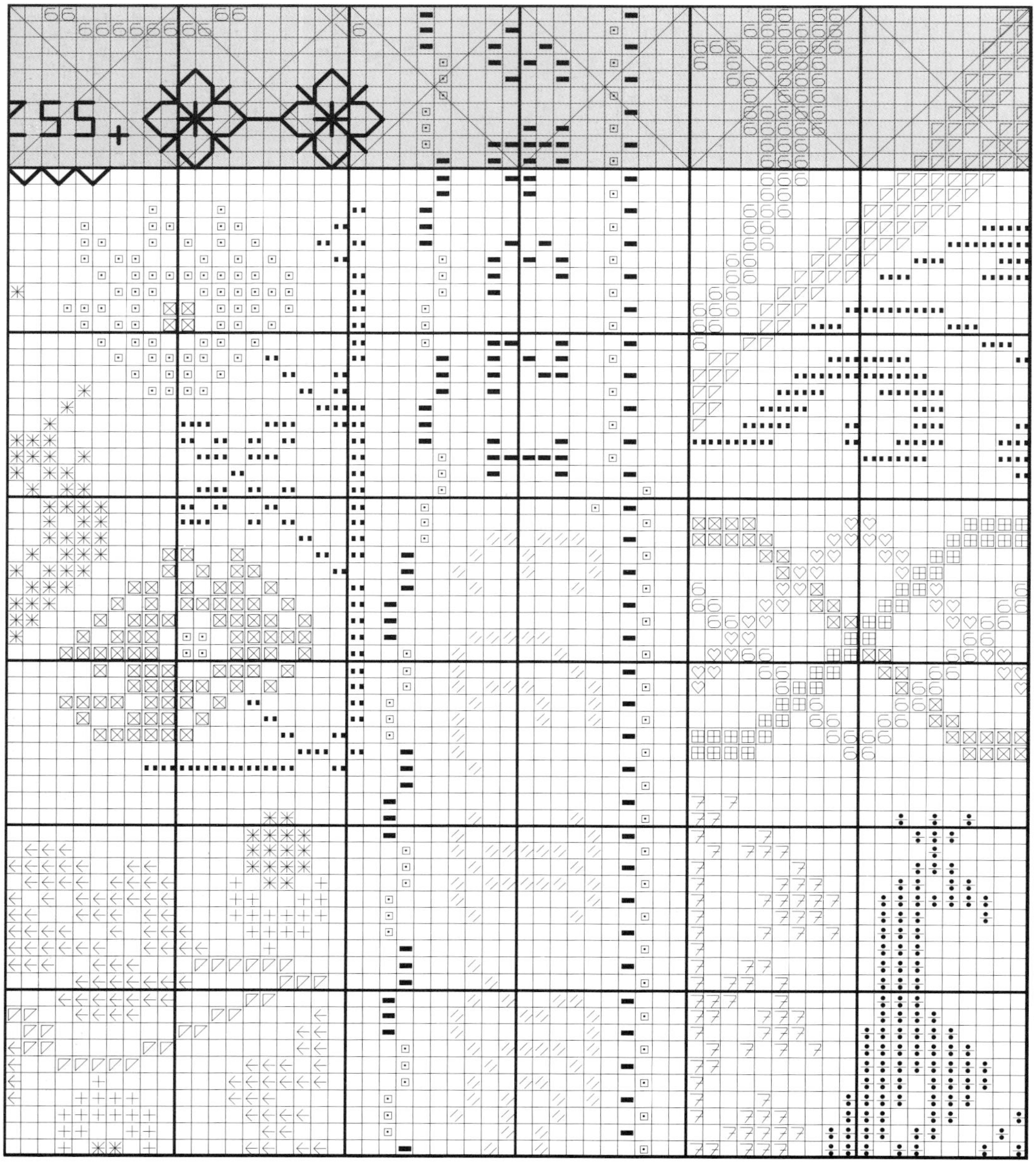

Central Band - 2

Shaded area indicates overlap from previous page

Refer to the colour photograph page 42 for additional detail

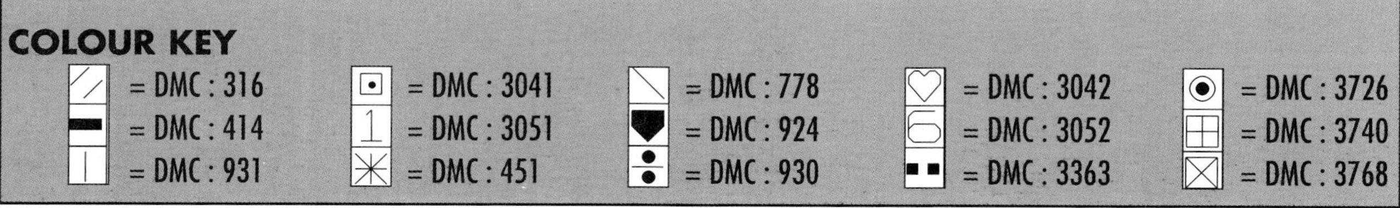

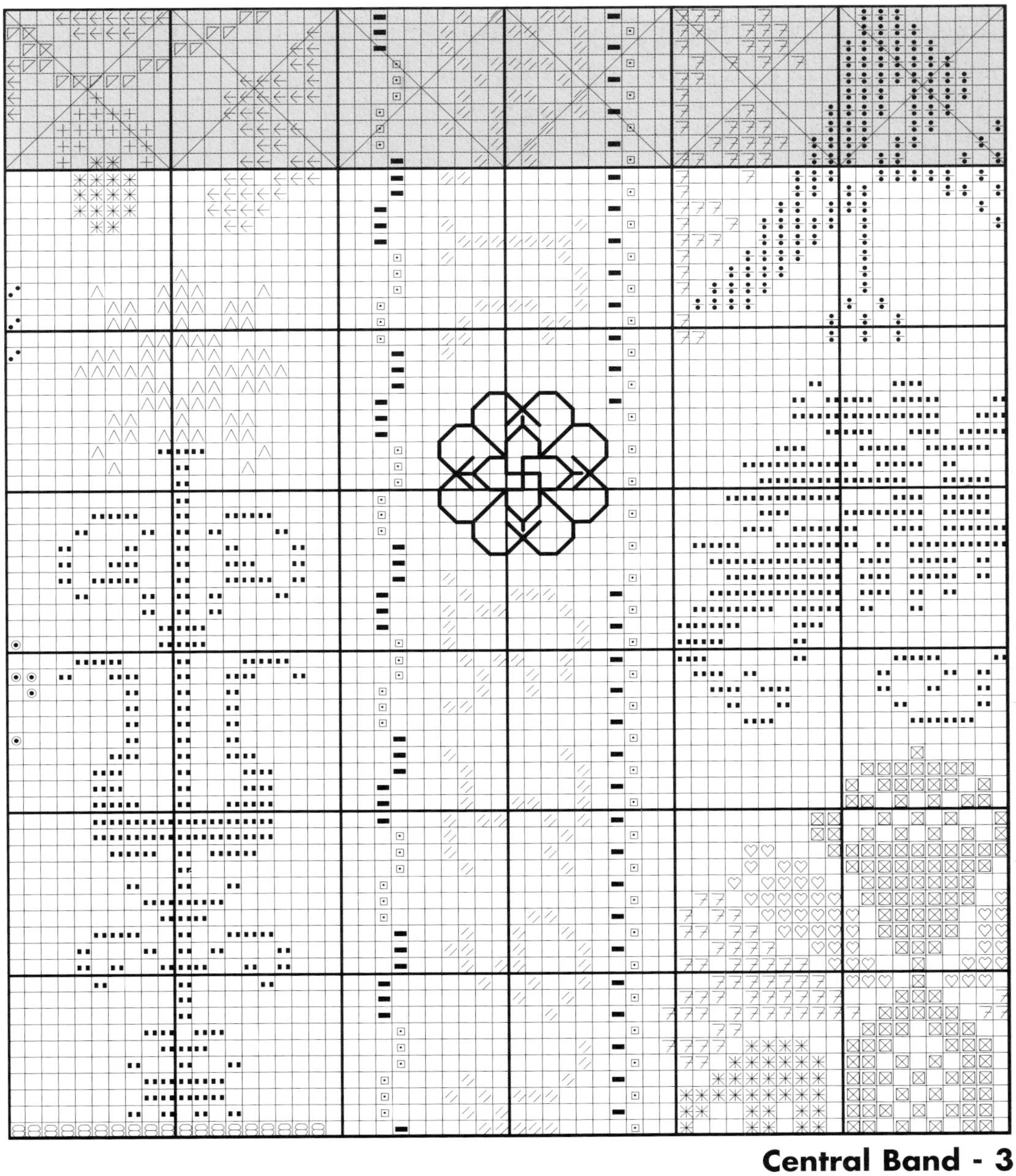

Central Band - 3

Shaded area indicates overlap from previous page
Refer to the colour photograph page 42 for additional detail

COLOUR KEY continued

= DMC : 3802	= DMC : 926	= DMC : 927	= DMC : 502	= DMC : 3347
= DMC : 3362	= DMC : 223	= DMC : 221	= DMC : 935	= DMC : 435
= DMC : 3727	= DMC : 988	= DMC : 452	= DMC : 932	

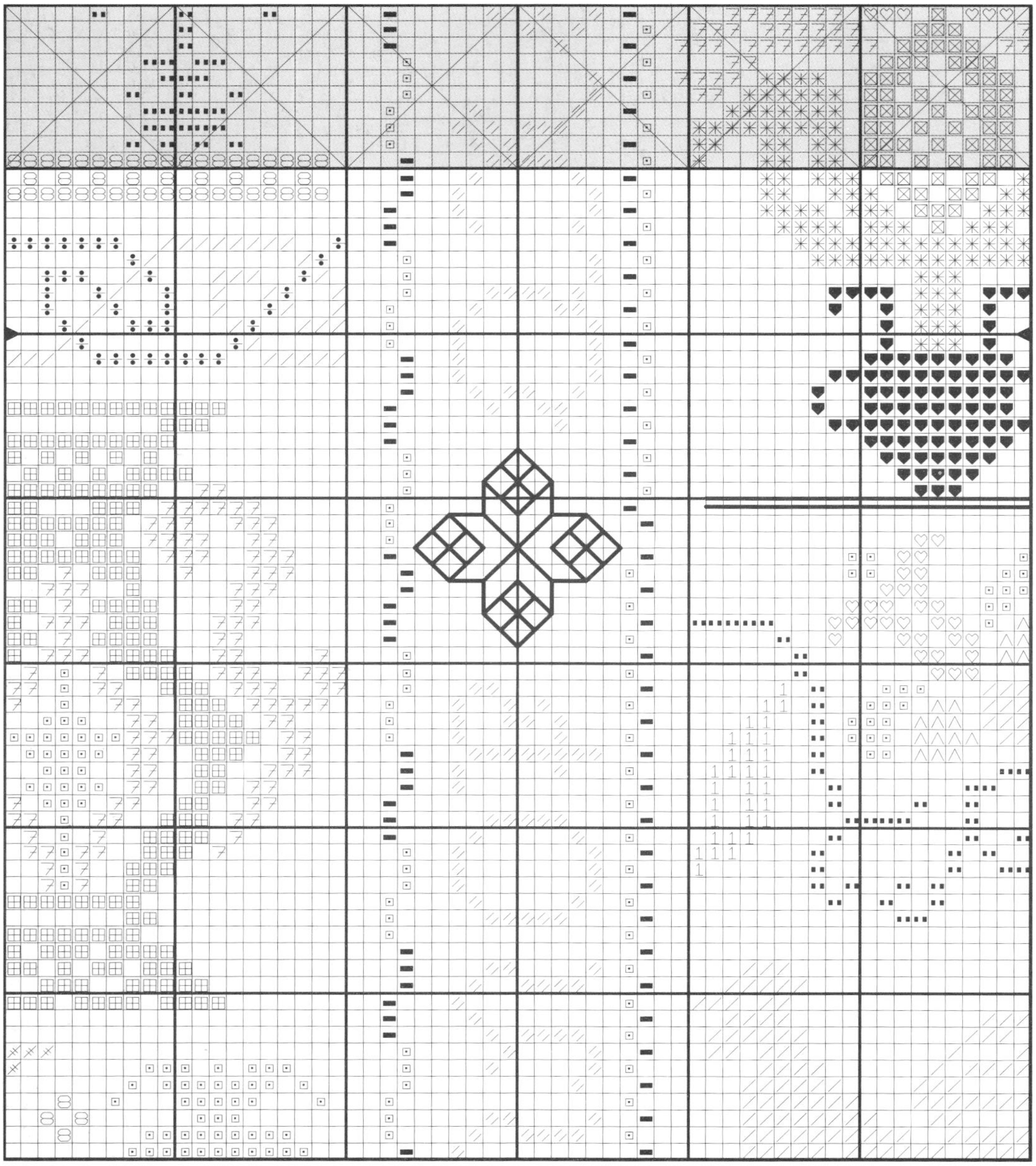

Central Band - 4

Shaded area indicates overlap from previous page
Refer to the colour photograph page 43 for additional detail

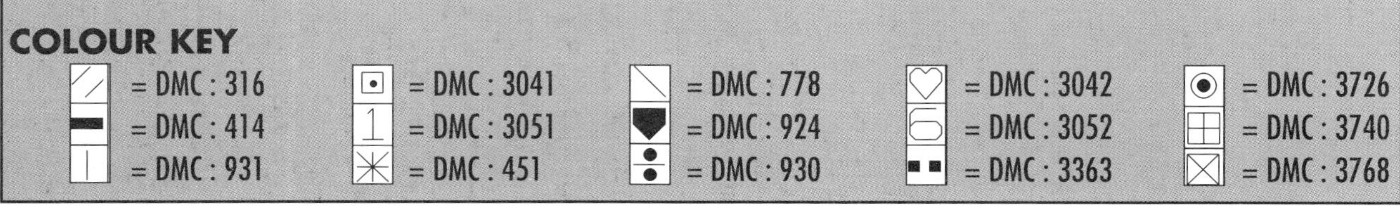

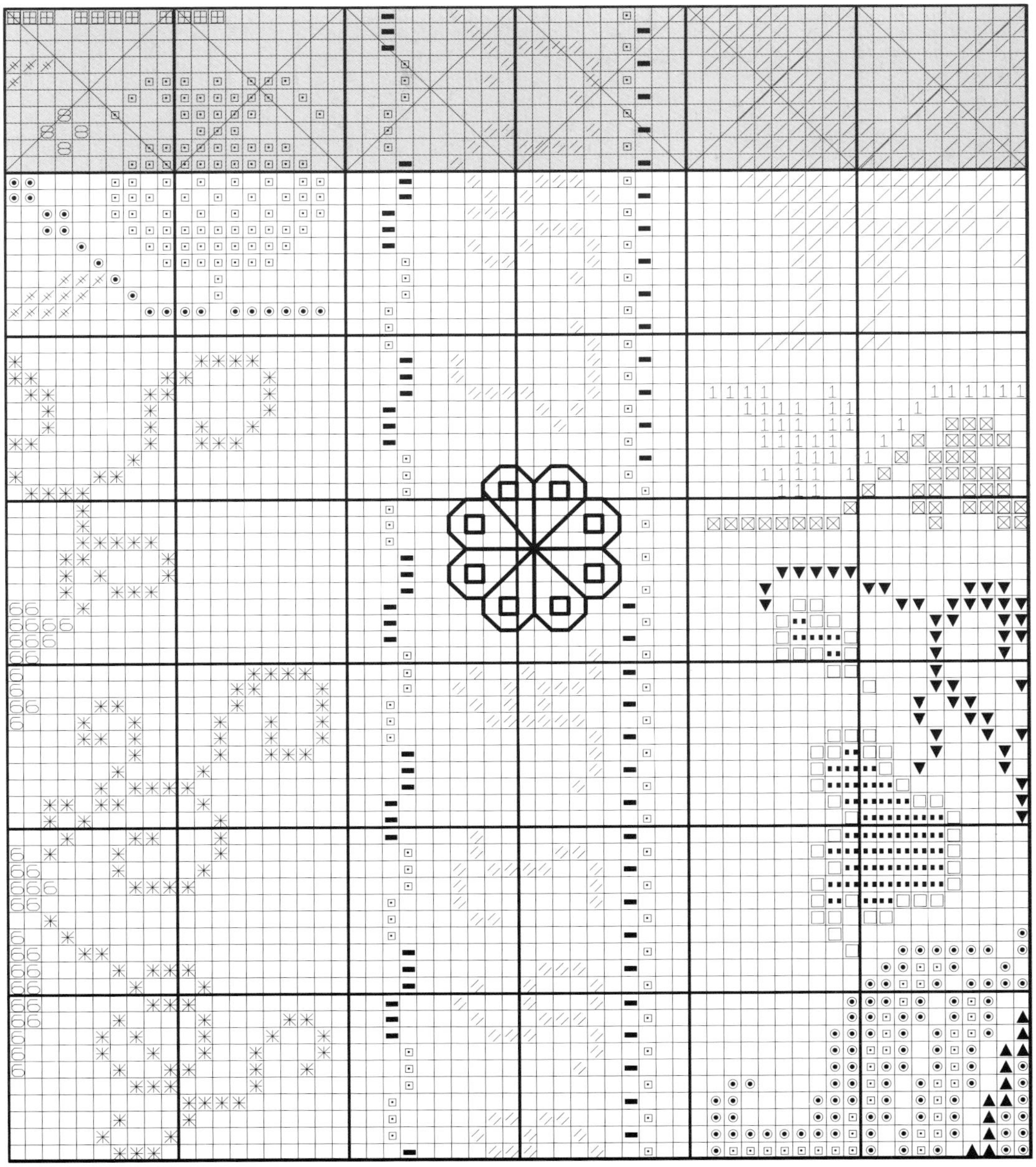

Central Band - 5

Shaded area indicates overlap from previous page
Refer to the colour photograph page 43 for additional detail

COLOUR KEY continued

= DMC : 3802	= DMC : 926	= DMC : 927	= DMC : 502	= DMC : 3347
= DMC : 3362	= DMC : 223	= DMC : 221	= DMC : 935	= DMC : 435
= DMC : 3727	= DMC : 988	= DMC : 452	= DMC : 932	

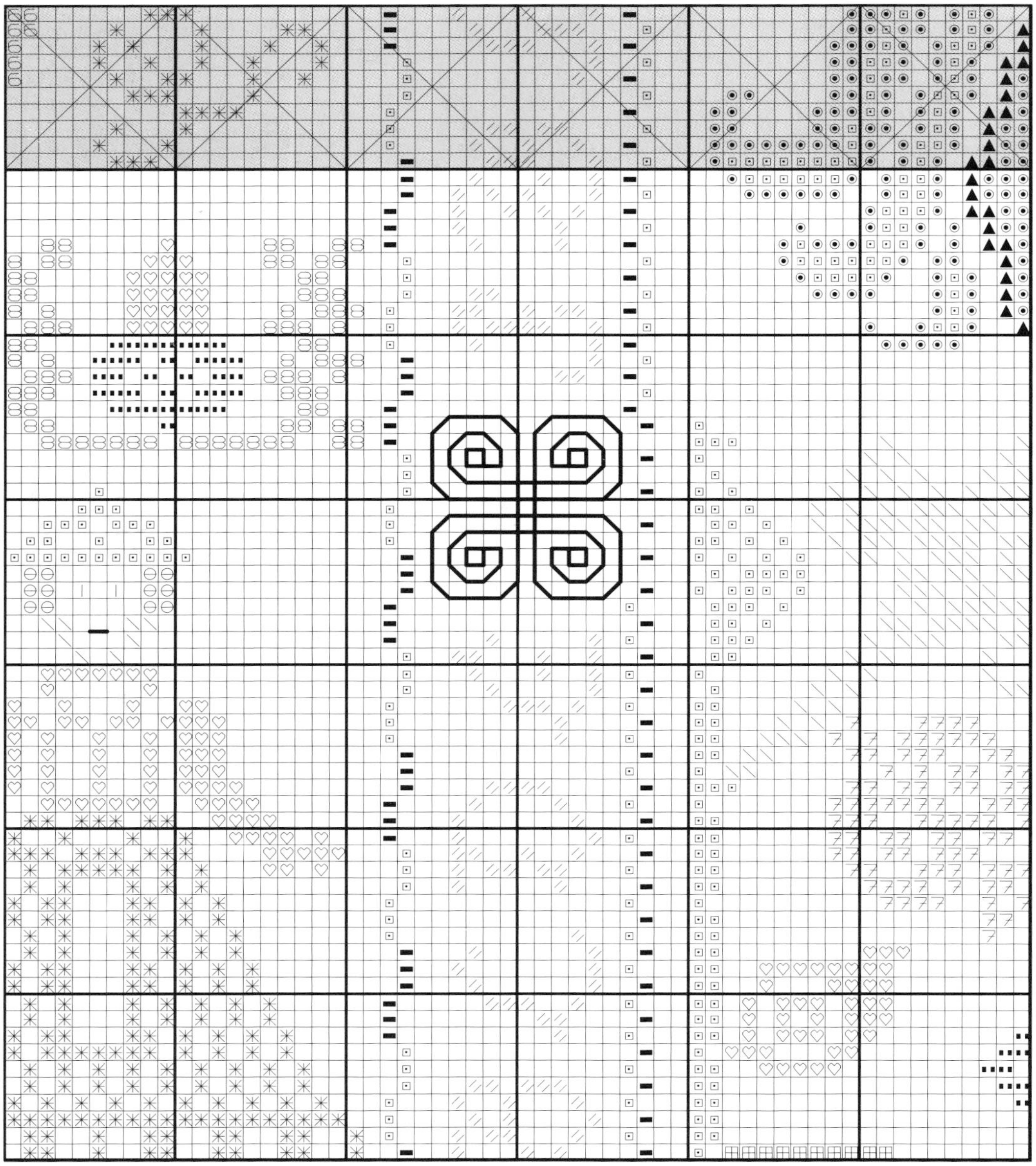

Central Band - 6

Shaded area indicates overlap from previous page
Refer to the colour photograph page 43 for additional detail

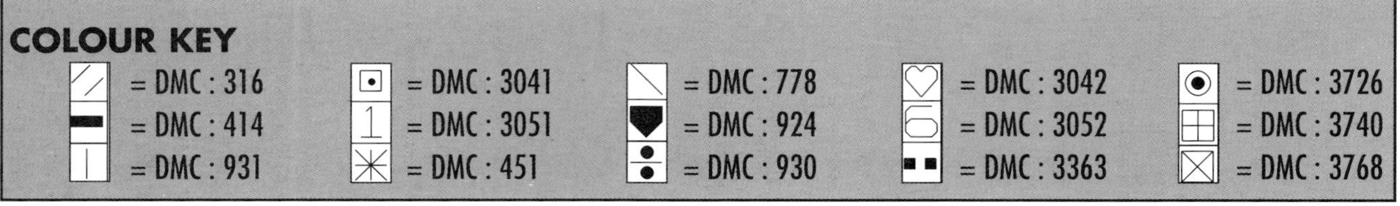

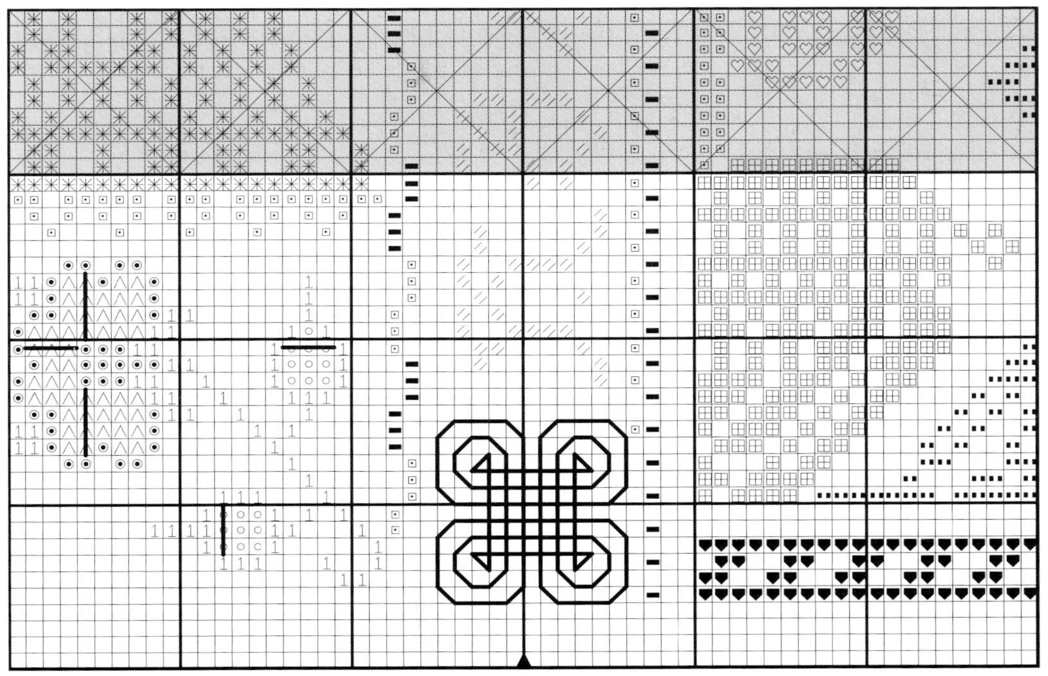

Central Band - 7

Shaded area indicates overlap from previous page

Refer to the colour photograph page 43 for additional detail

COLOUR KEY continued

Symbol	DMC	Symbol	DMC	Symbol	DMC	Symbol	DMC	Symbol	DMC
╱	= DMC : 3802	8	= DMC : 926	••	= DMC : 927	○	= DMC : 502	←	= DMC : 3347
◸	= DMC : 3362	∧	= DMC : 223	▲	= DMC : 221	▼	= DMC : 935	⊖	= DMC : 435
⅂	= DMC : 3727	✕	= DMC : 988	+	= DMC : 452	□	= DMC : 932		

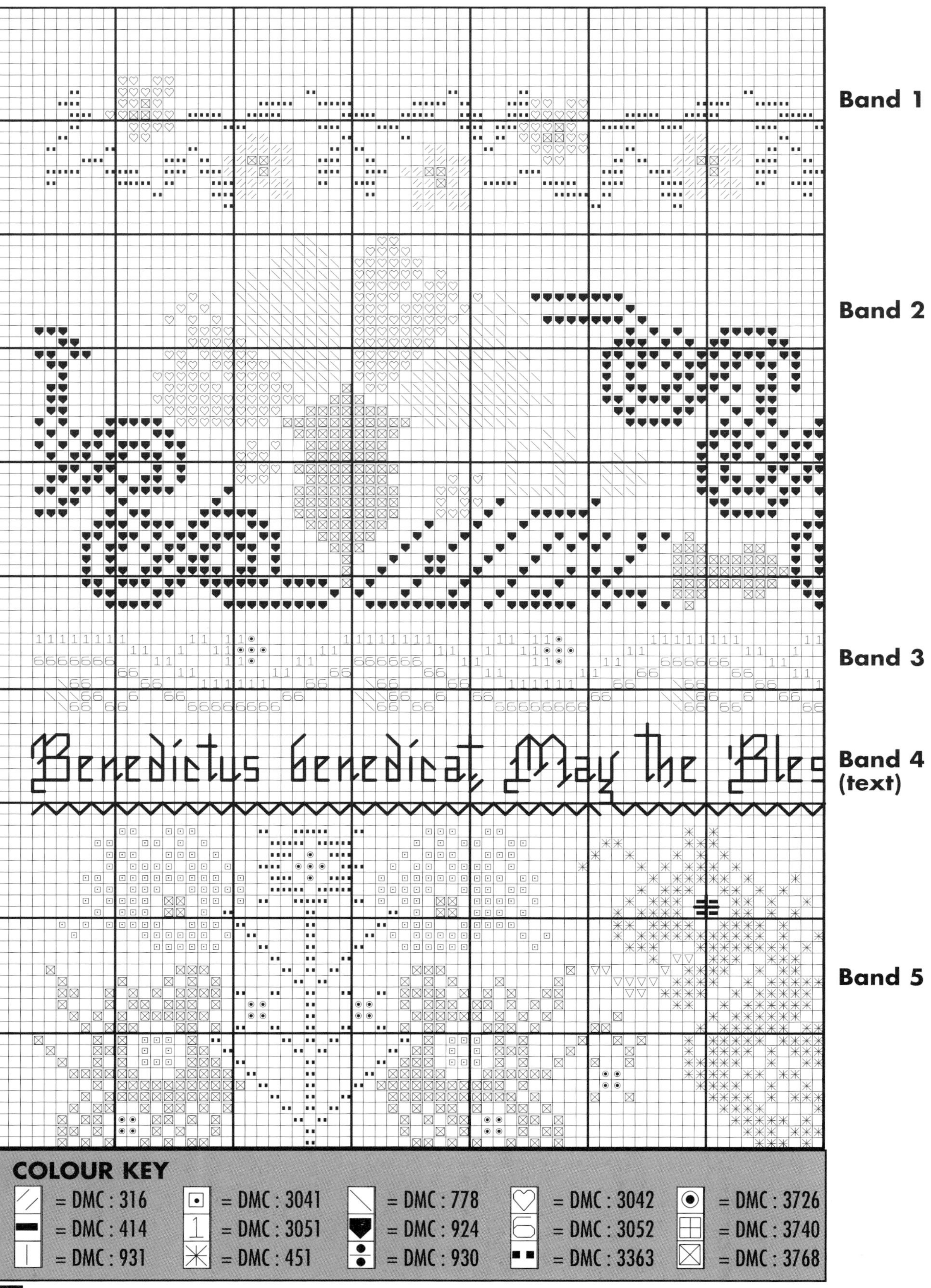

Band 1

Band 2

Band 3

Band 4 (text)

Band 5

Top Section - left hand side of Double Band Sampler
Band 1 - part of band 5

Refer to the colour photograph page 42 for additional detail

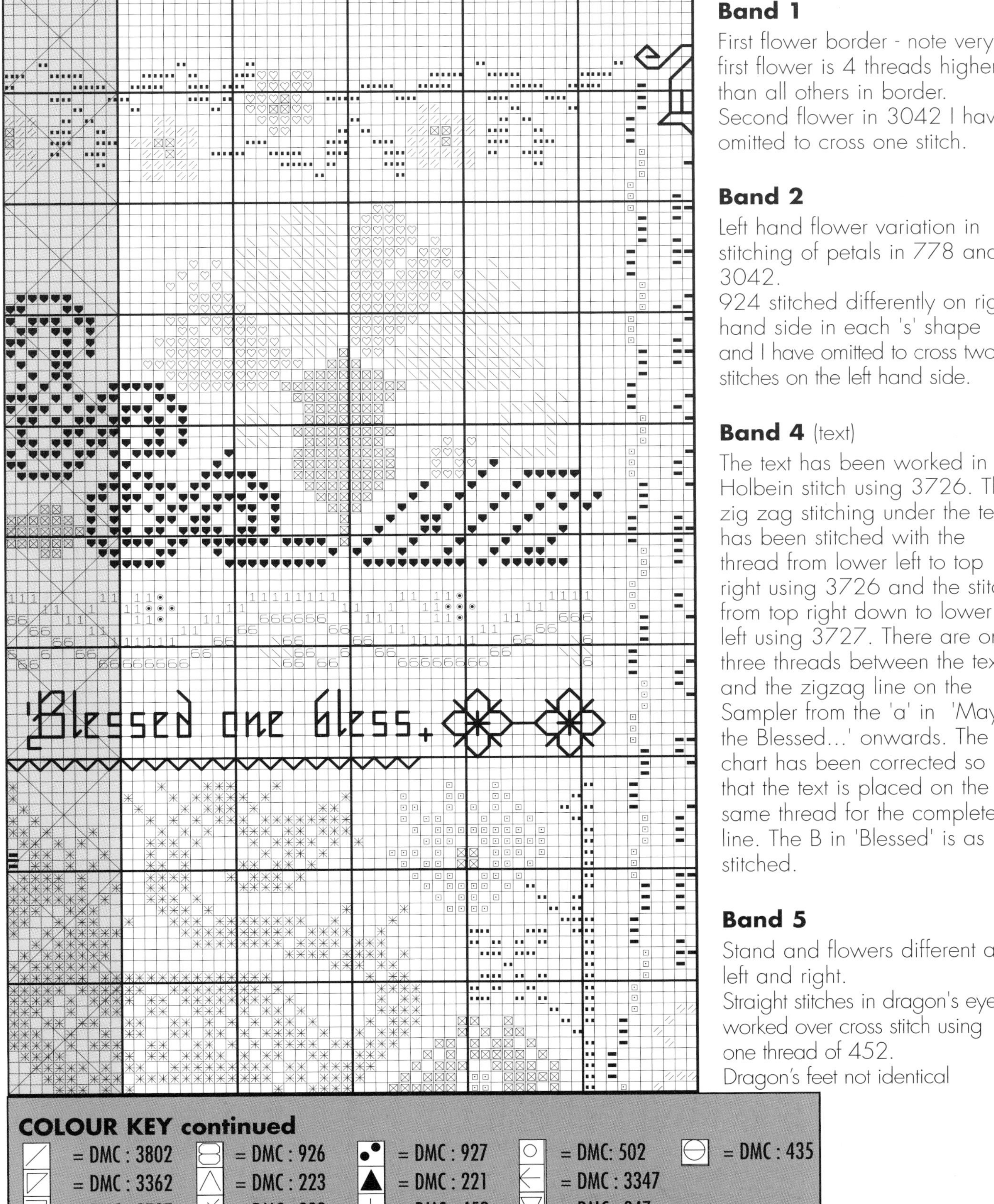

LEFT HAND SIDE BORDERS

Band 1

First flower border - note very first flower is 4 threads higher than all others in border. Second flower in 3042 I have omitted to cross one stitch.

Band 2

Left hand flower variation in stitching of petals in 778 and 3042.
924 stitched differently on right hand side in each 's' shape and I have omitted to cross two stitches on the left hand side.

Band 4 (text)

The text has been worked in Holbein stitch using 3726. The zig zag stitching under the text has been stitched with the thread from lower left to top right using 3726 and the stitch from top right down to lower left using 3727. There are only three threads between the text and the zigzag line on the Sampler from the 'a' in 'May the Blessed...' onwards. The chart has been corrected so that the text is placed on the same thread for the complete line. The B in 'Blessed' is as stitched.

Band 5

Stand and flowers different at left and right.
Straight stitches in dragon's eye worked over cross stitch using one thread of 452.
Dragon's feet not identical

COLOUR KEY continued

Symbol	DMC	Symbol	DMC	Symbol	DMC	Symbol	DMC	Symbol	DMC
⁄	= DMC : 3802	8	= DMC : 926	●•	= DMC : 927	○	= DMC: 502	⊖	= DMC : 435
◸	= DMC : 3362	△	= DMC : 223	▲	= DMC : 221	←	= DMC : 3347		
7	= DMC : 3727	×	= DMC : 988	+	= DMC : 452	▽	= DMC : 347		

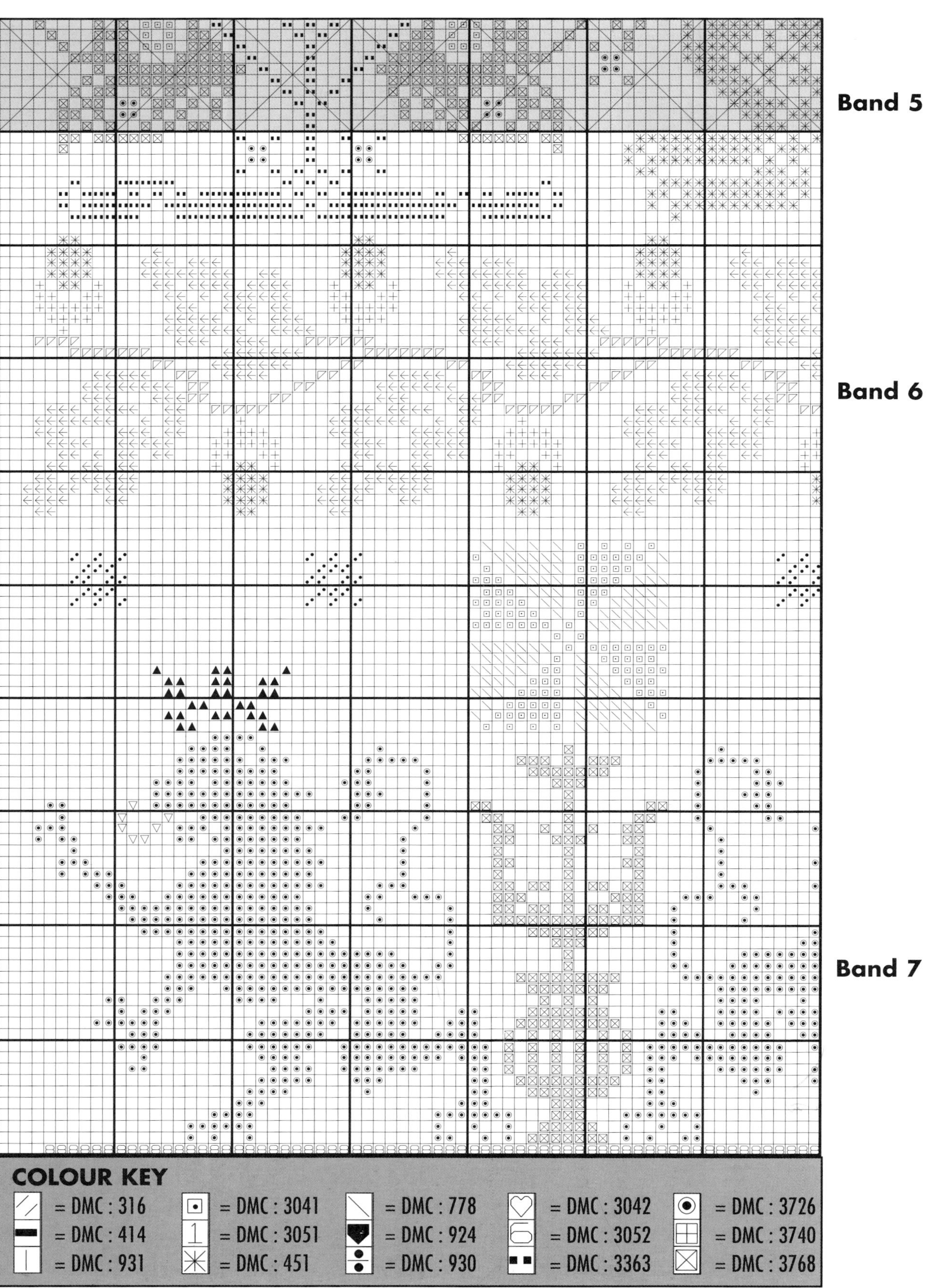

Band 5
Band 6
Band 7
COLOUR KEY
= DMC : 316
= DMC : 414
= DMC : 931
= DMC : 3041
= DMC : 3051
= DMC : 451
= DMC : 778
= DMC : 924
= DMC : 930
= DMC : 3042
= DMC : 3052
= DMC : 3363
= DMC : 3726
= DMC : 3740
= DMC : 3768

Second Section - left hand side of Double Band Sampler
Rest of band 5 - part of band 7

Shaded areas indicate overlaps from previous page
Refer to the colour photograph page 42 for additional detail

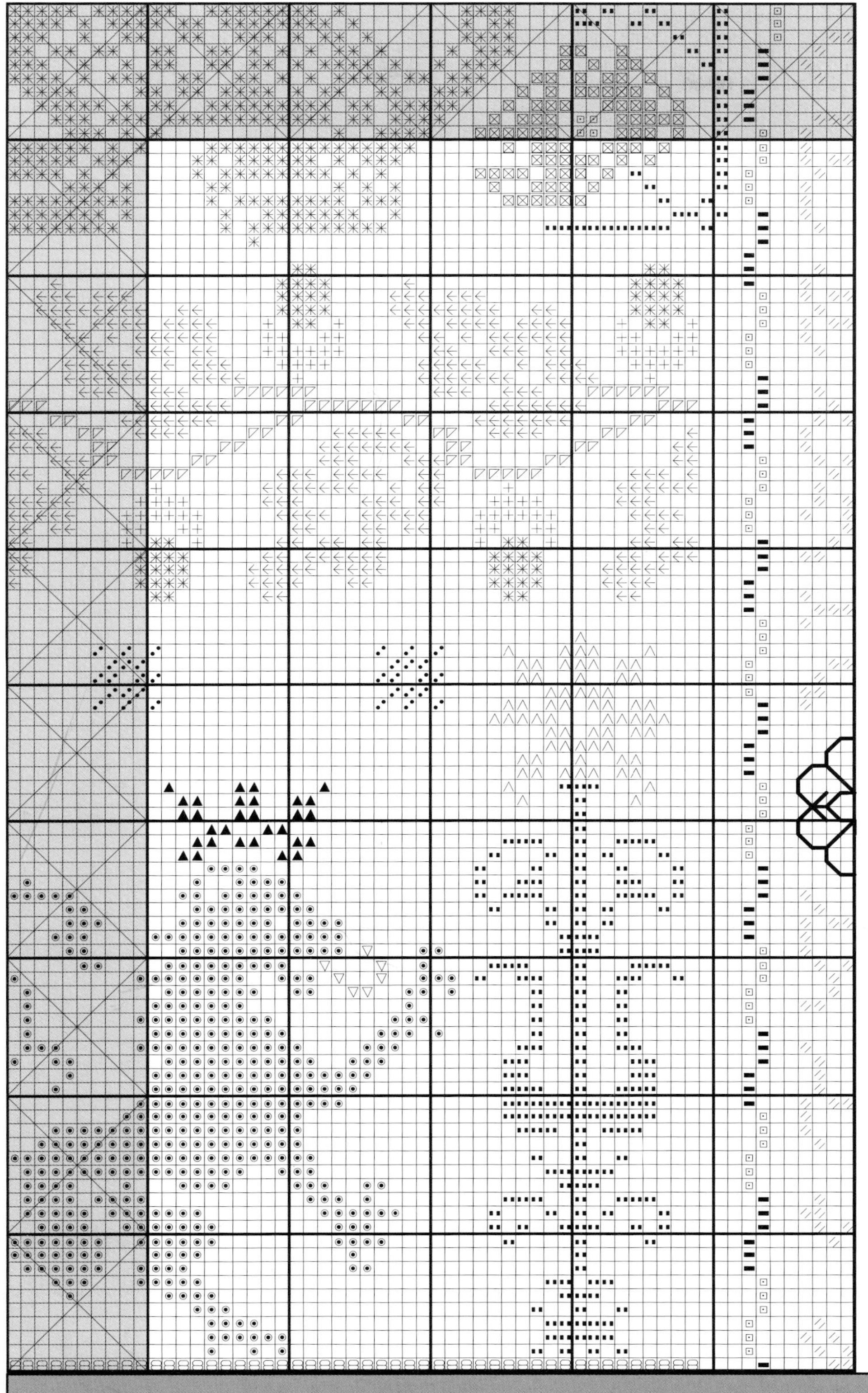

Band 6
Placement of second acorn from left, lower row, different from others.
Lower first leaf is very slightly different from the others.

Band 7
Left lion's feet stitched differently to those of right lion.
Flower in pot is asymmetrical, variation in central petal left hand side in 223.
Not all leaf stitches have been crossed in original sampler.

COLOUR KEY continued

Symbol	DMC	Symbol	DMC	Symbol	DMC	Symbol	DMC	Symbol	DMC
⁄	= DMC : 3802	8	= DMC : 926	•:	= DMC : 927	○	= DMC: 502	⊖	= DMC : 435
◸	= DMC : 3362	△	= DMC : 223	▲	= DMC : 221	←	= DMC : 3347		
⁷	= DMC : 3727	⨯	= DMC : 988	+	= DMC : 452	▽	= DMC : 347		

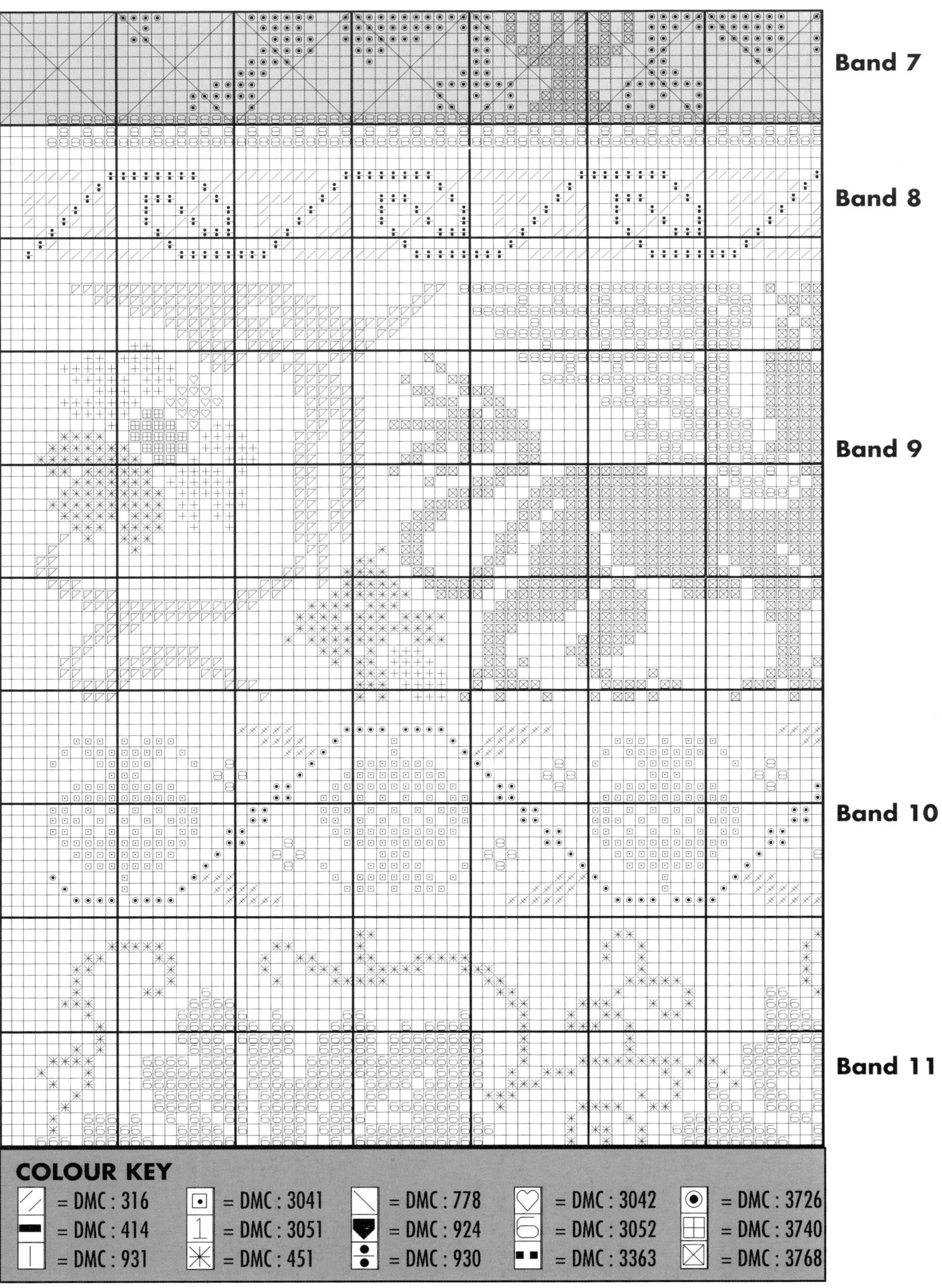
Band 7
Band 8
Band 9
Band 10
Band 11
COLOUR KEY
= DMC : 316
= DMC : 414
= DMC : 931
= DMC : 3041
= DMC : 3051
= DMC : 451
= DMC : 778
= DMC : 924
= DMC : 930
= DMC : 3042
= DMC : 3052
= DMC : 3363
= DMC : 3726
= DMC : 3740
= DMC : 3768

Third Section - left hand side of Double Band Sampler
Rest of band 7 - top of band 11

Shaded areas indicate overlaps from previous page

Refer to the colour photograph page 43 for additional detail

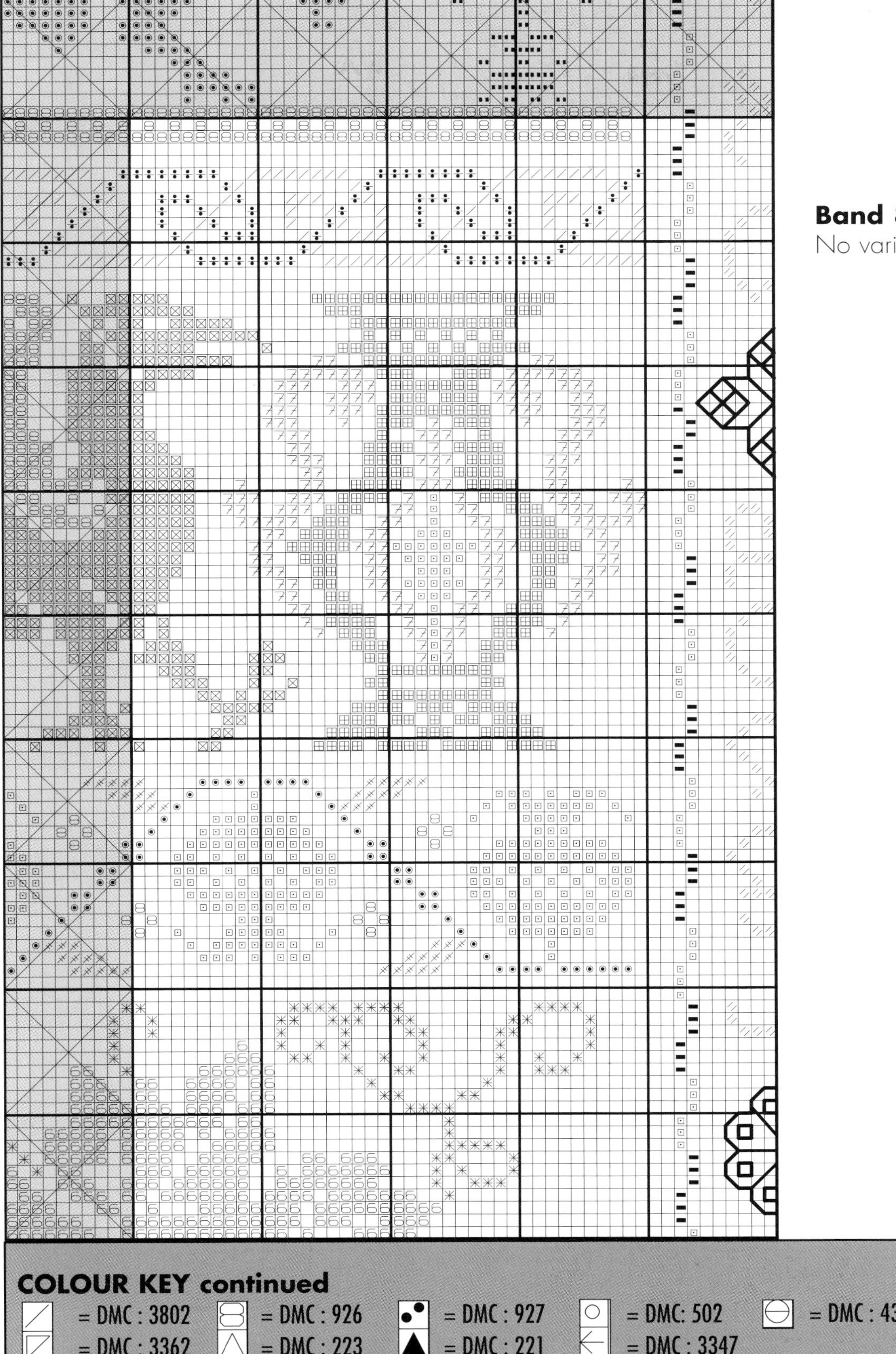

Band 8, 9, 10 & 11

No variations

COLOUR KEY continued

Symbol	DMC	Symbol	DMC	Symbol	DMC	Symbol	DMC	Symbol	DMC
╱	= DMC : 3802	8	= DMC : 926	••	= DMC : 927	○	= DMC: 502	⊖	= DMC : 435
◸	= DMC : 3362	∧	= DMC : 223	▲	= DMC : 221	←	= DMC : 3347		
⁊	= DMC : 3727	×	= DMC : 988	+	= DMC : 452	▽	= DMC : 347		

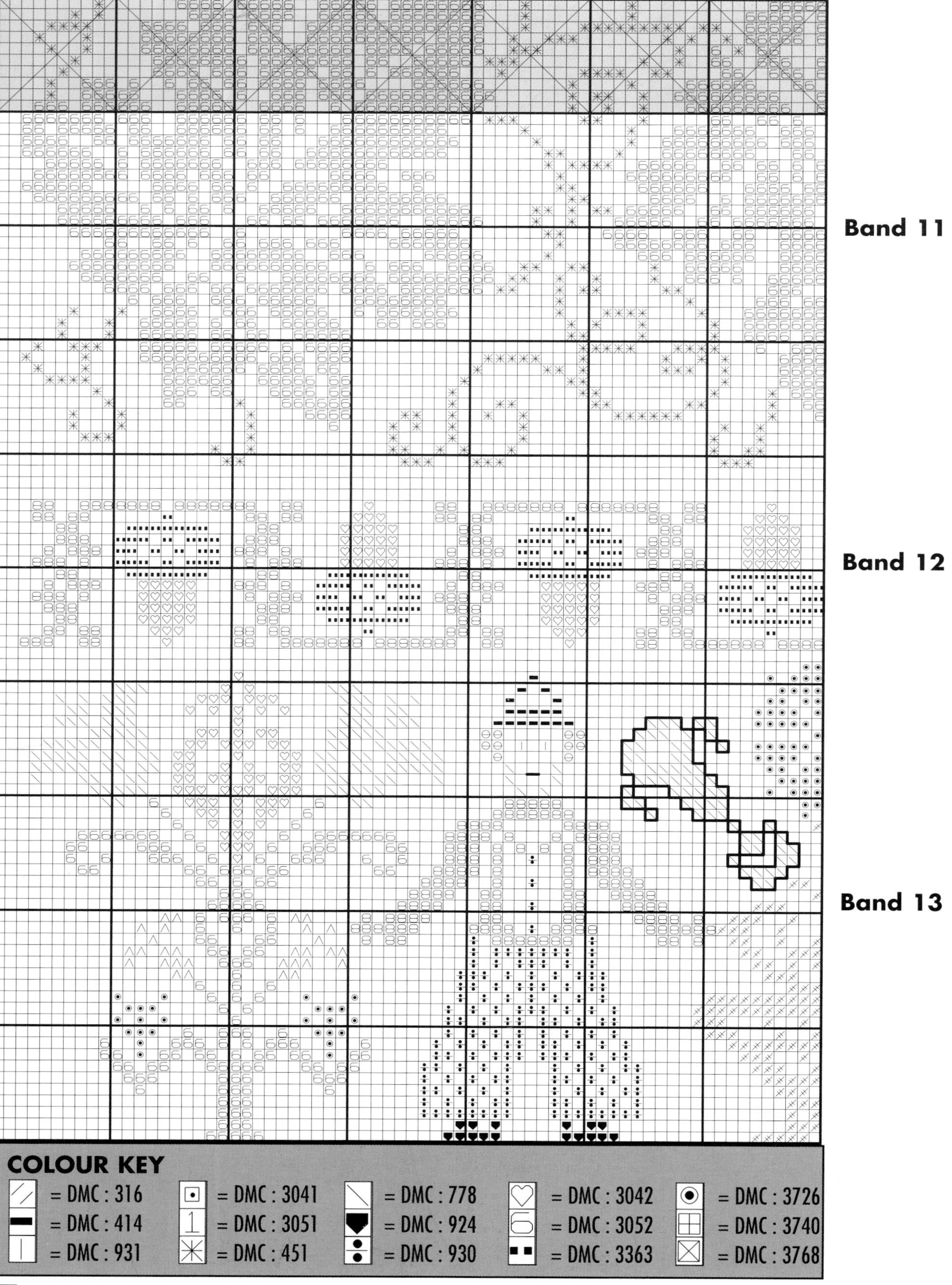

COLOUR KEY

/	= DMC : 316	⊡	= DMC : 3041	\	= DMC : 778	♡	= DMC : 3042	⊙	= DMC : 3726
▬	= DMC : 414	1	= DMC : 3051	♥	= DMC : 924	6	= DMC : 3052	⊞	= DMC : 3740
|	= DMC : 931	✳	= DMC : 451	:	= DMC : 930	▪▪	= DMC : 3363	⊠	= DMC : 3768

Fourth Section - left hand side of Double Band Sampler
Rest of band 11- most of band 13

Shaded areas indicate overlaps from previous page
Refer to the colour photograph page 43 for additional detail

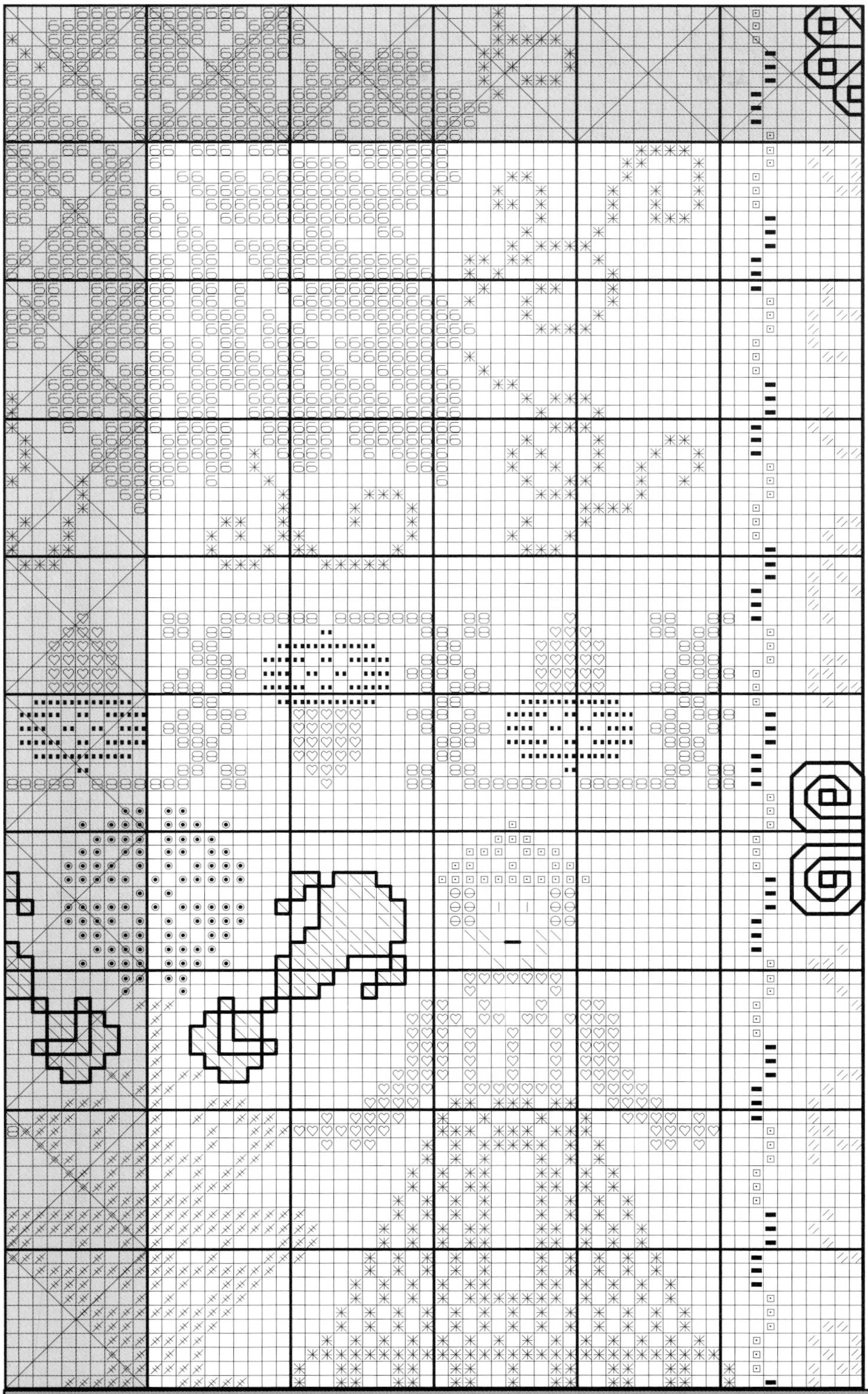

Band 13 (Boy and girl)
Mouth one straight stitch worked in 347.
Eyes are one cross stitch back stitched on all four sides.
Top flowers between two figures are outlined in Holbein stitch using one thread of 451.

COLOUR KEY continued

= DMC : 3802	= DMC : 926	= DMC : 927	= DMC: 502	= DMC : 435
= DMC : 3362	= DMC : 223	= DMC : 221	= DMC : 3347	
= DMC : 3727	= DMC : 988	= DMC : 452	= DMC : 347	

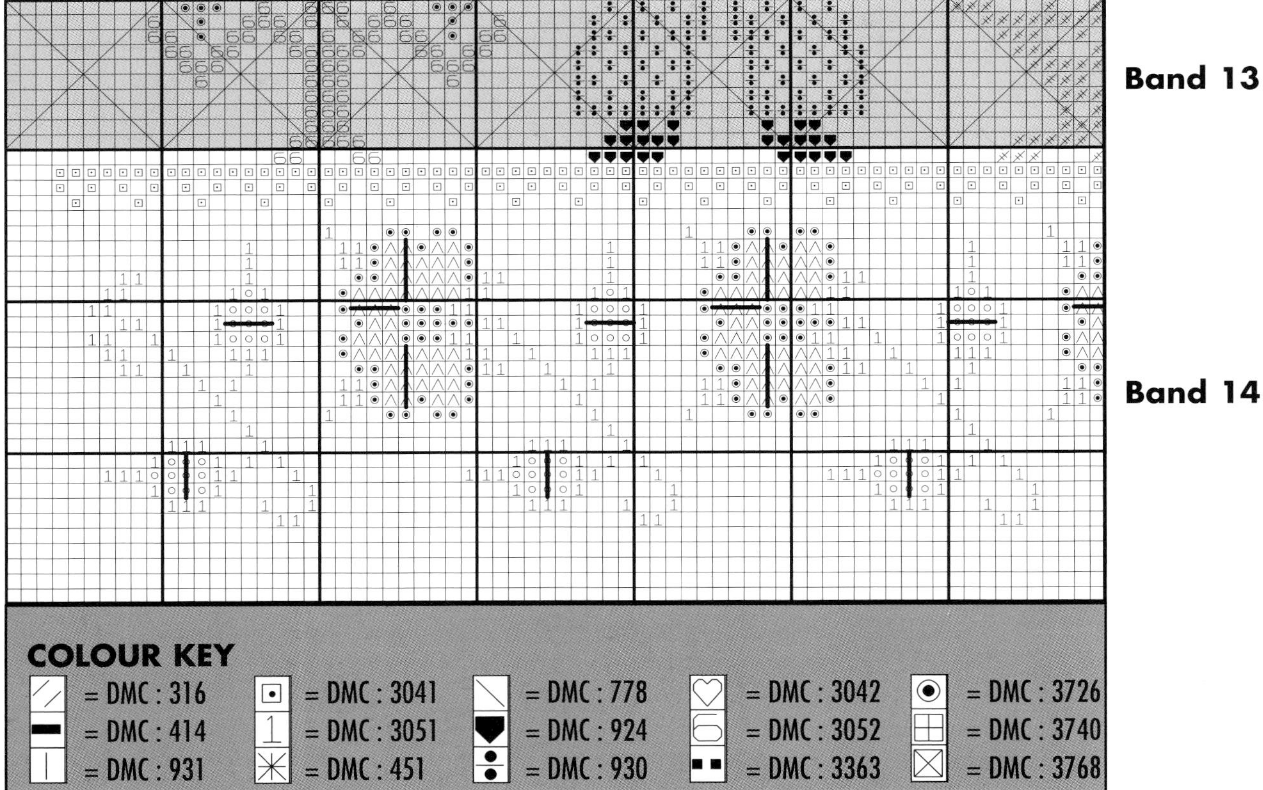
Band 13
Band 14
COLOUR KEY
= DMC : 316
= DMC : 414
= DMC : 931
= DMC : 3041
= DMC : 3051
= DMC : 451
= DMC : 778
= DMC : 924
= DMC : 930
= DMC : 3042
= DMC : 3052
= DMC : 3363
= DMC : 3726
= DMC : 3740
= DMC : 3768

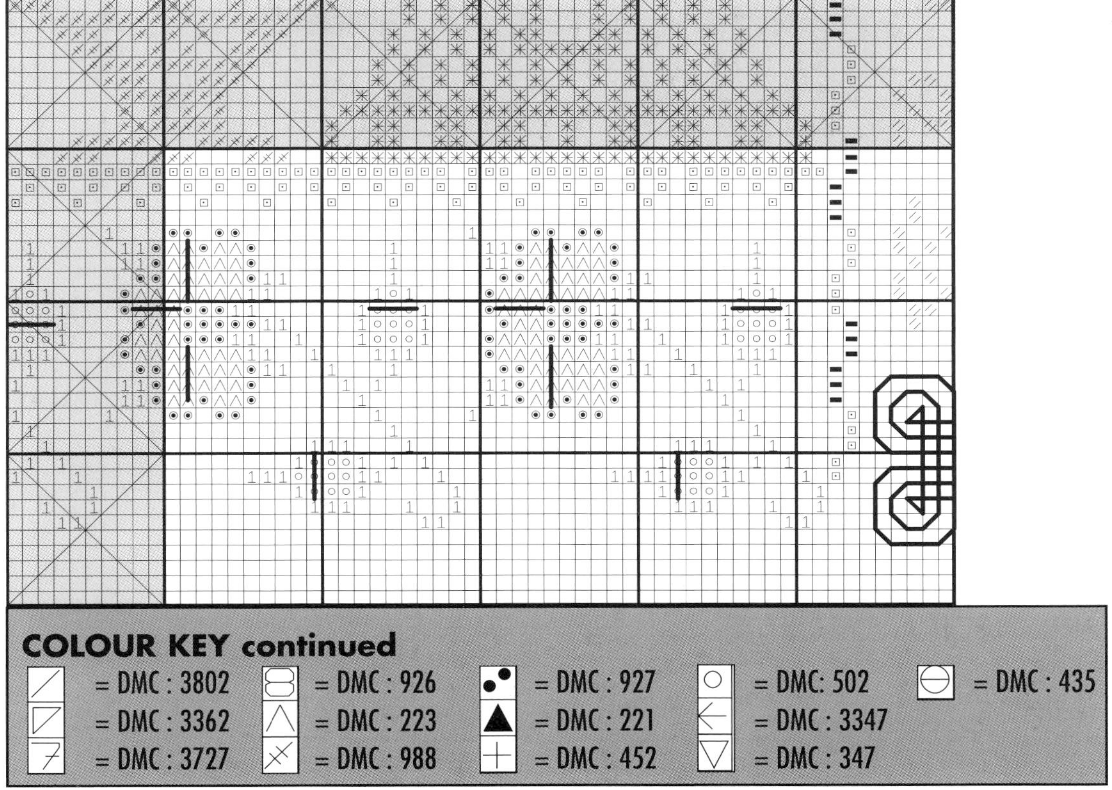

COLOUR KEY continued
= DMC : 3802
= DMC : 3362
= DMC : 3727
= DMC : 926
= DMC : 223
= DMC : 988
= DMC : 927
= DMC : 221
= DMC : 452
= DMC: 502
= DMC : 3347
= DMC : 347
= DMC : 435

Fifth Section - left hand side of Double Band Sampler
Rest of band 13 and band 14

Shaded areas indicate overlaps from previous page

Refer to the colour photograph page 43 for additional detail

Band 14 In the flowers the vertical satin stitch is worked over more threads than the horizontal satin stitch. Satin stitch is worked using two threads of 223 in the direction of the straight lines. The leaves are worked in satin stitch using 502. The top leaves are stitched horizontally and the lower leaves are stitched vertically.

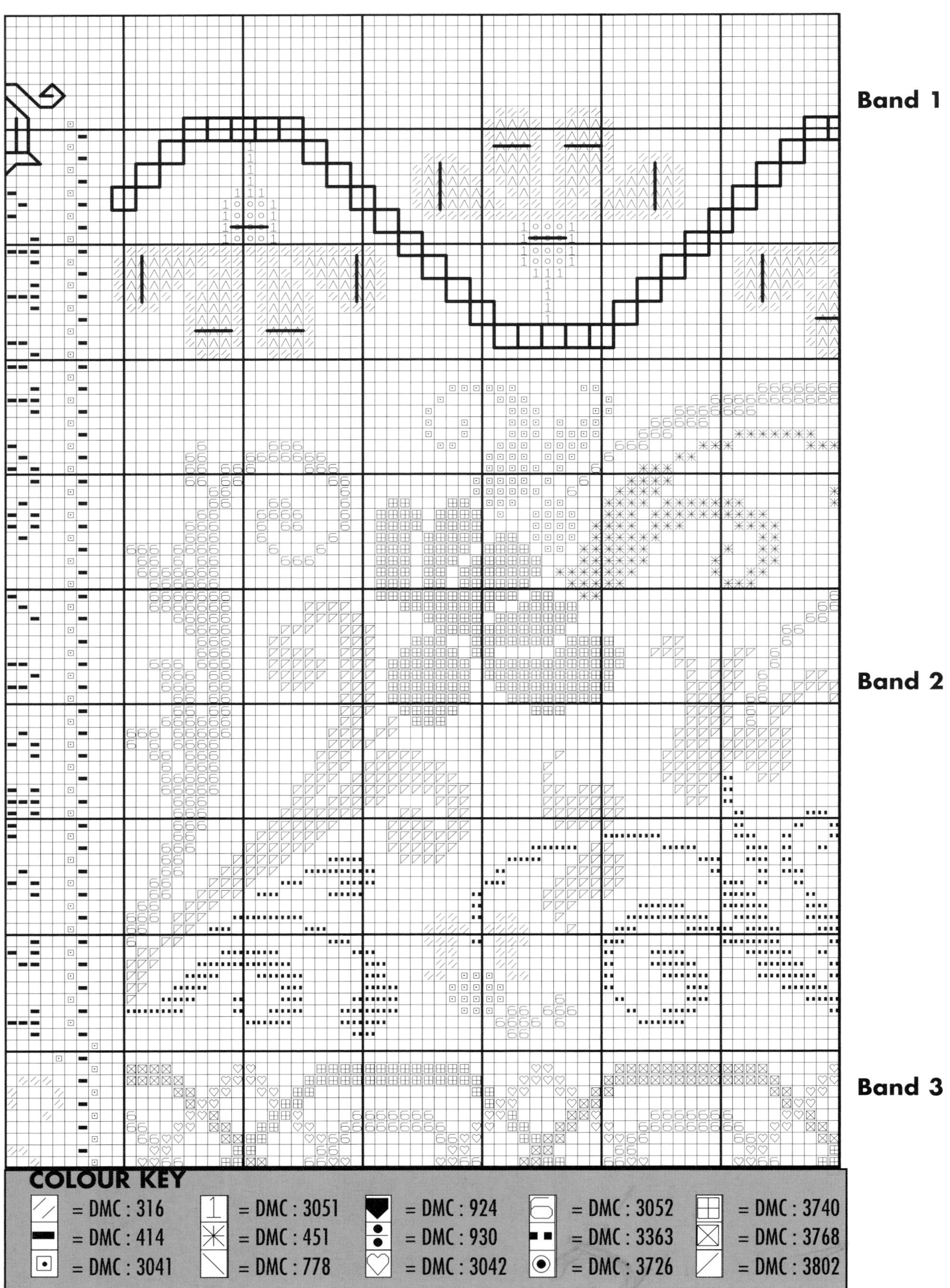
Band 1
Band 2
Band 3
COLOUR KEY
= DMC : 316
= DMC : 414
= DMC : 3041
= DMC : 3051
= DMC : 451
= DMC : 778
= DMC : 924
= DMC : 930
= DMC : 3042
= DMC : 3052
= DMC : 3363
= DMC : 3726
= DMC : 3740
= DMC : 3768
= DMC : 3802

Top Section - right hand side of Double Band Sampler
Band 1 - part of band 3

Refer to the colour photograph page 44 for additional detail

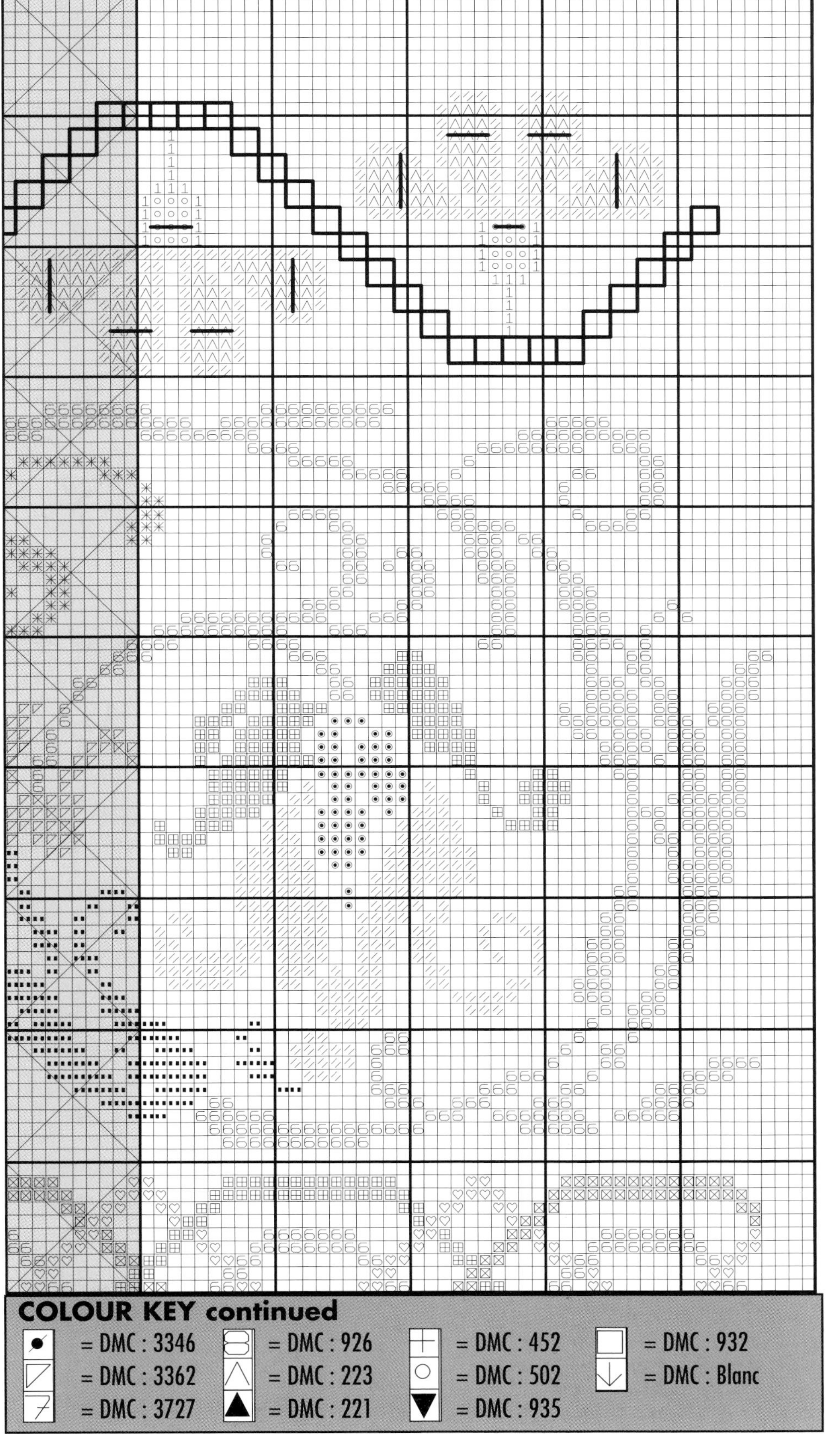

Shaded area indicates overlap from previous chart

Band 1

Square boxes represent eyelet stitch worked over four threads in each direction using one thread of 926.
Satin stitch worked in direction of straight lines using two threads of 223 for the flower petals and two threads of 502 for the calyx.

Band 2

This is an asymmetrical pattern, stitch carefully. I really enjoy the subtle variations in shades of green in this design.

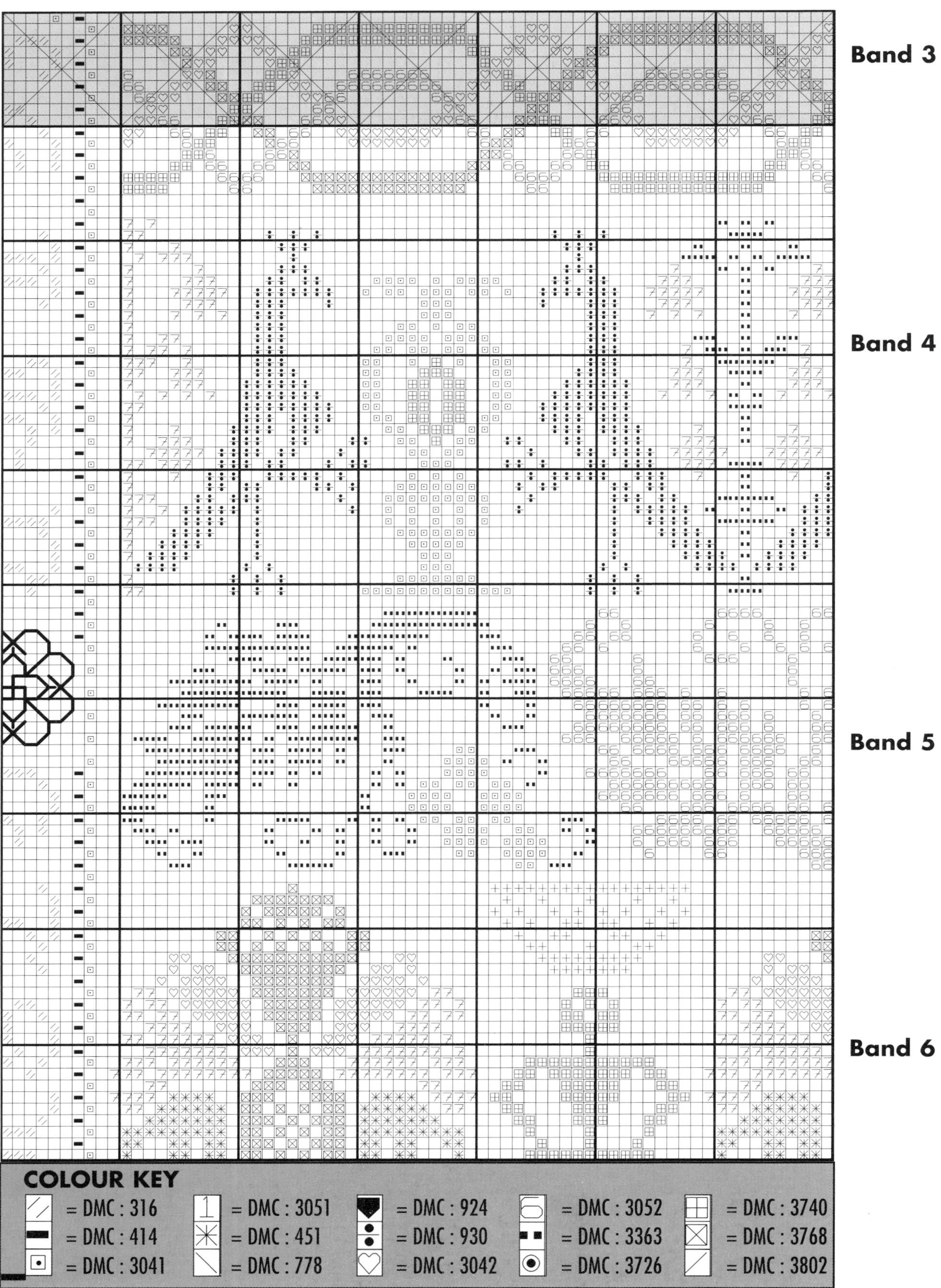

COLOUR KEY

⁄	= DMC : 316	⊥	= DMC : 3051	♥ (filled)	= DMC : 924	6	= DMC : 3052	⊞	= DMC : 3740
▬	= DMC : 414	✳	= DMC : 451	⁝	= DMC : 930	▪▪	= DMC : 3363	⊠	= DMC : 3768
⊡	= DMC : 3041	╲	= DMC : 778	♡	= DMC : 3042	◉	= DMC : 3726	╱	= DMC : 3802

Second Section - right hand side of Double Band Sampler
Rest of band 3 - part of band 6

Shaded areas indicates overlaps from previous page

Refer to the colour photograph page 44 - 45 for additional detail

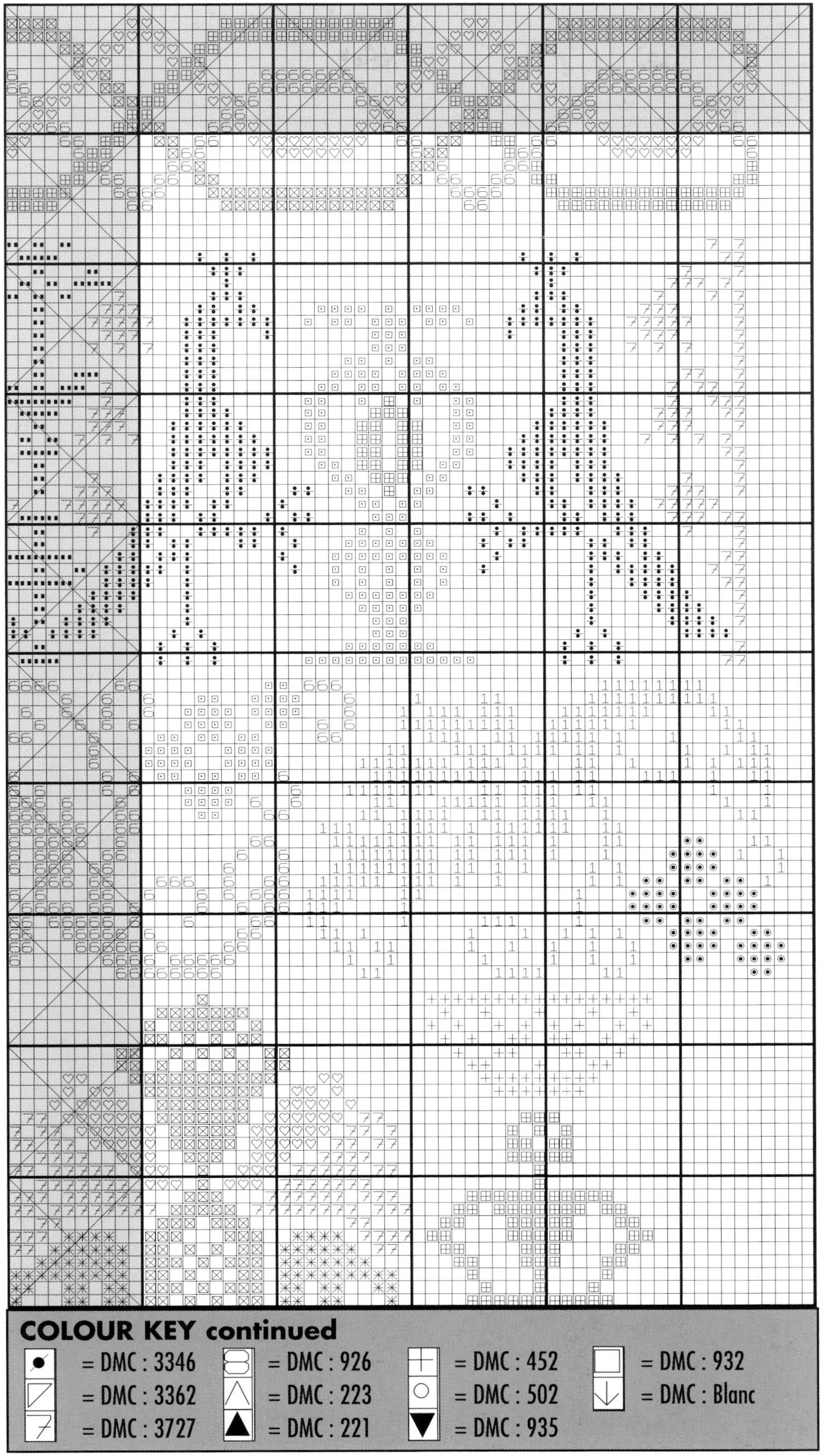

COLOUR KEY continued

●	= DMC : 3346	8	= DMC : 926	+	= DMC : 452	□	= DMC : 932
◸	= DMC : 3362	△	= DMC : 223	○	= DMC : 502	↓	= DMC : Blanc
7	= DMC : 3727	▲	= DMC : 221	▼	= DMC : 935		

Band 4

Slight variation in 3727 between both ends

Variation in foot of third eagle

Band 5

No variations

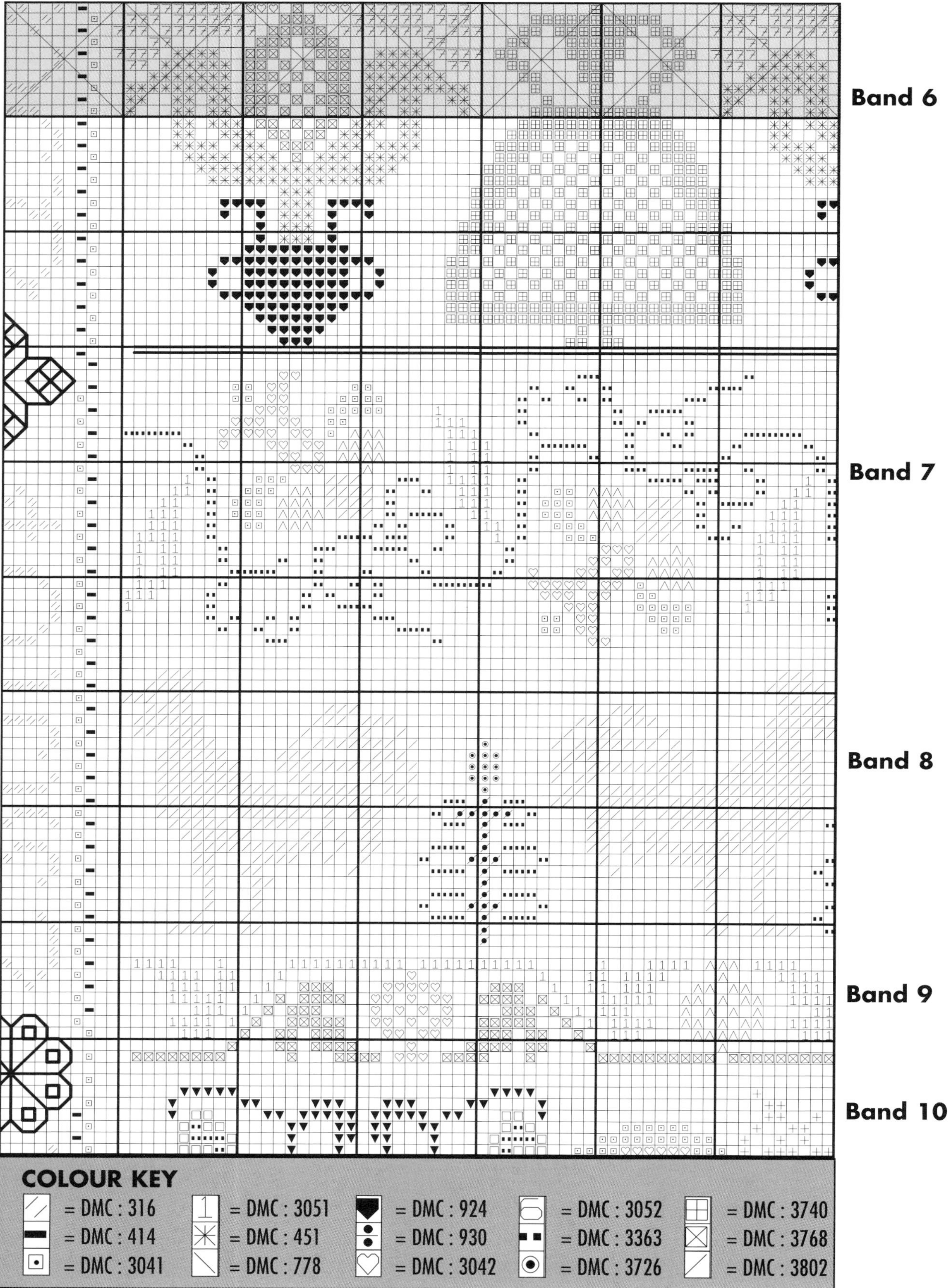

COLOUR KEY

= DMC : 316	= DMC : 3051	= DMC : 924	= DMC : 3052	= DMC : 3740
= DMC : 414	= DMC : 451	= DMC : 930	= DMC : 3363	= DMC : 3768
= DMC : 3041	= DMC : 778	= DMC : 3042	= DMC : 3726	= DMC : 3802

Third Section - right hand side of Double Band Sampler
Rest of band 6 - start of band 10

Shaded areas indicate overlaps from previous page
Refer to the colour photograph page 45 for additional detail

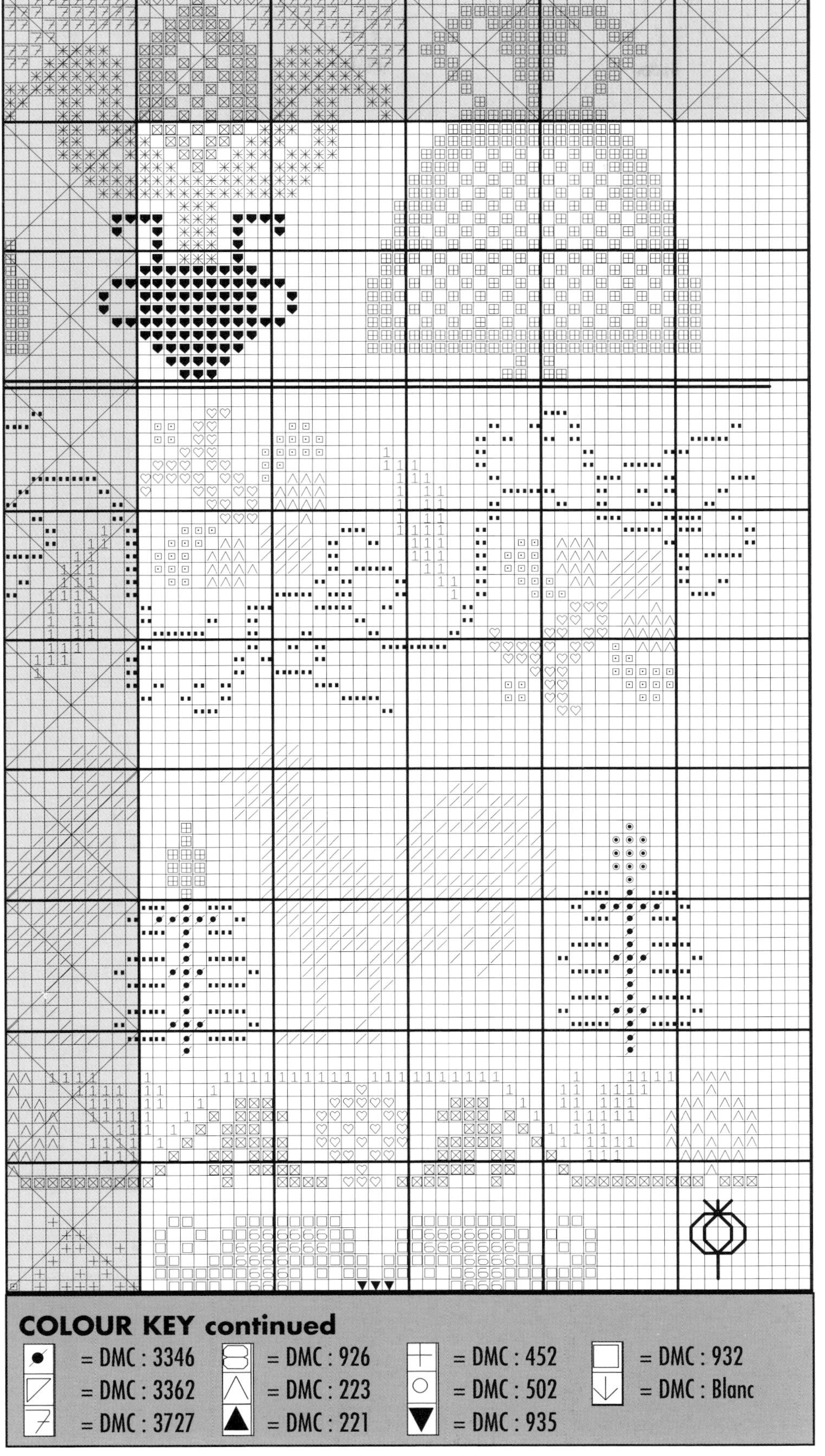

Band 6

The two rows of Holbein stitch underneath the two people are only one thread apart. The first row is stitched using one thread of 3768 and the second row is stitched using one thread of 924.

Band 8

Central flower placement and stitching different. Variable use of colour in leaves has been corrected.

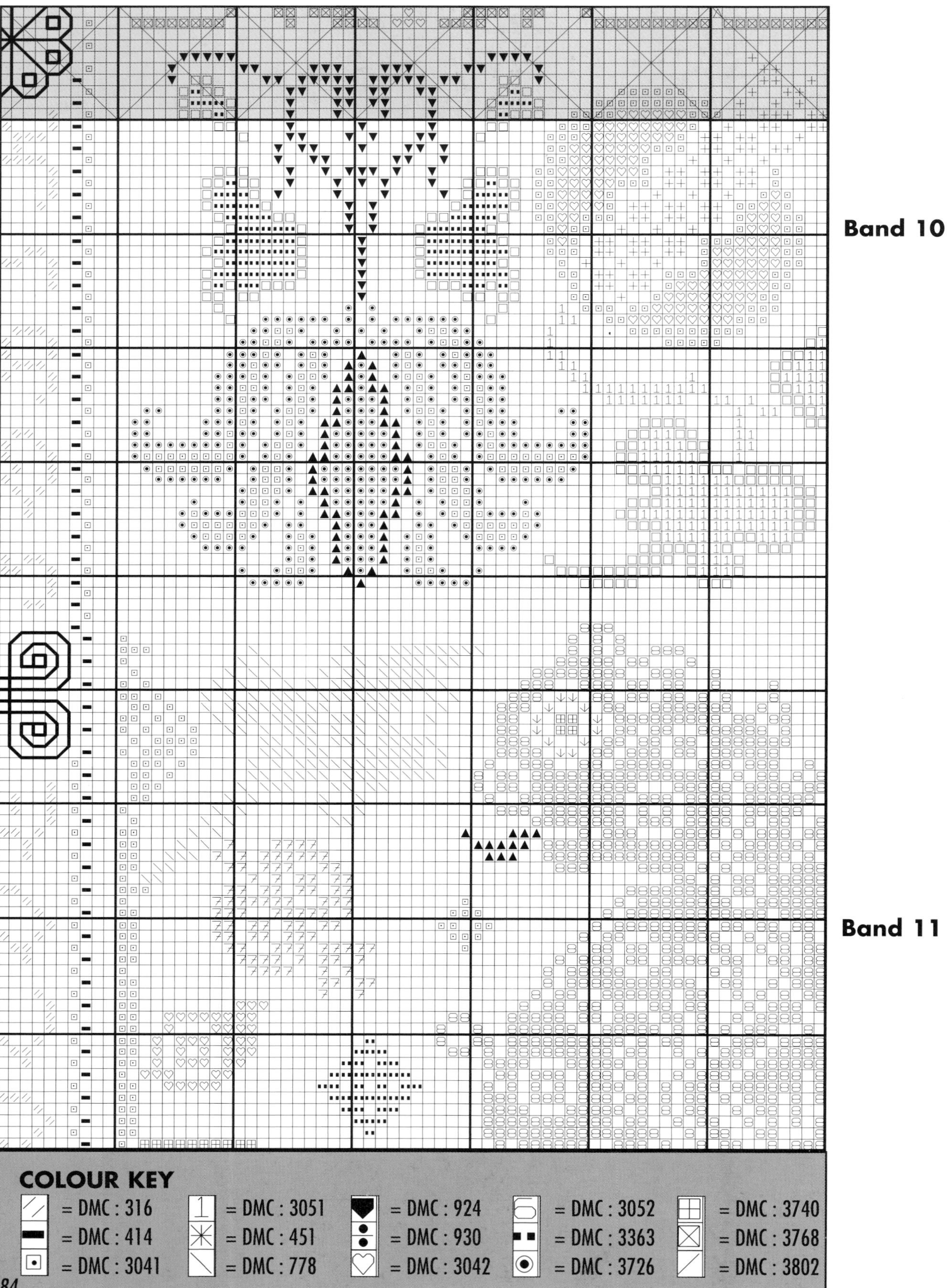
Band 10
Band 11
COLOUR KEY
= DMC : 316
= DMC : 414
= DMC : 3041
= DMC : 3051
= DMC : 451
= DMC : 778
= DMC : 924
= DMC : 930
= DMC : 3042
= DMC : 3052
= DMC : 3363
= DMC : 3726
= DMC : 3740
= DMC : 3768
= DMC : 3802

Fourth Section - right hand side of Double Band Sampler
Rest of band 10 - half of band 11

Shaded area indicatesoverlaps from previous page
Refer to the colour photograph page 46 for additional detail

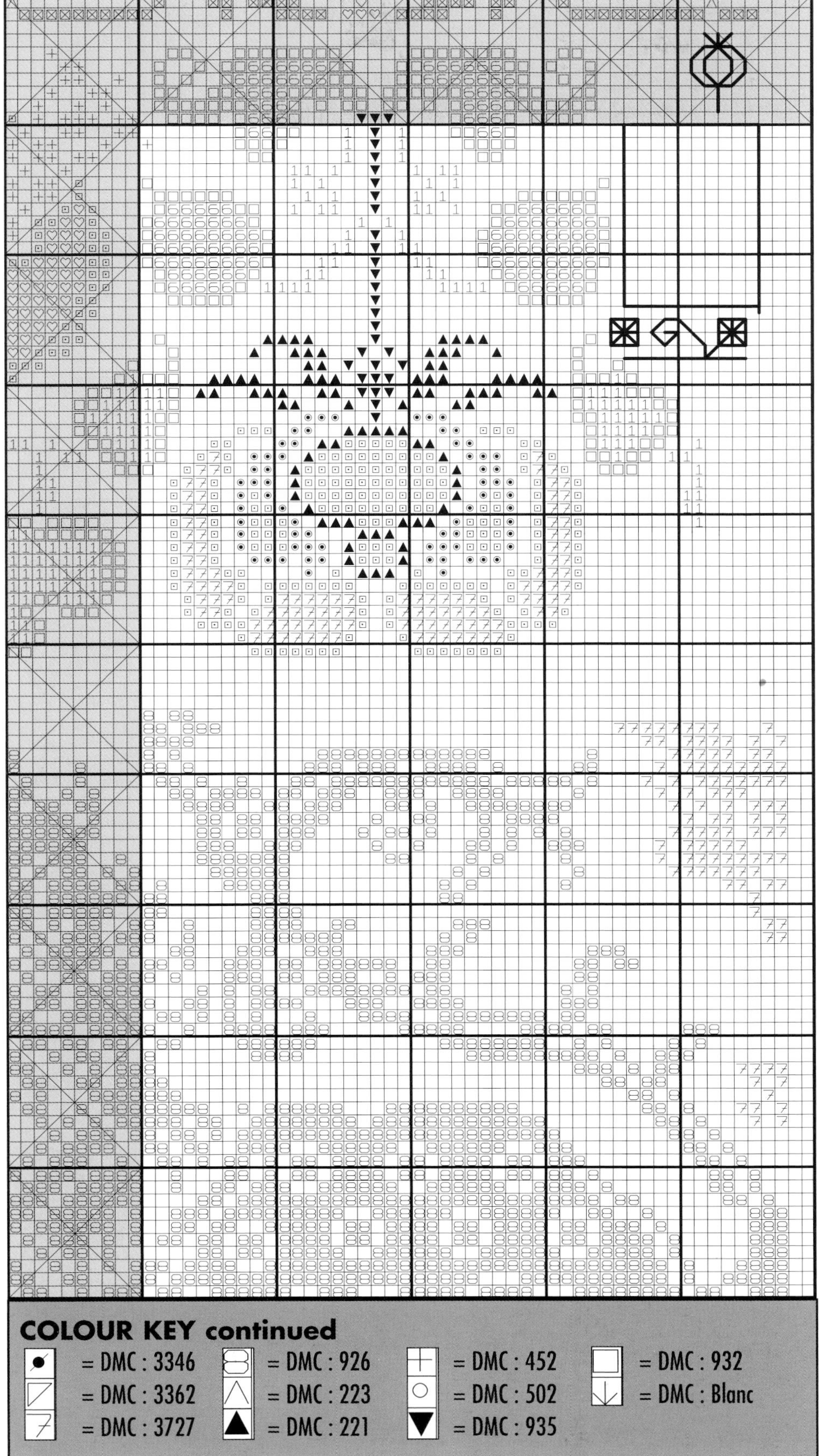

Band 10

There is room for your initials and date of completion here.
Note small leaves are asymmetrical.

COLOUR KEY continued

●	= DMC : 3346	8	= DMC : 926	+	= DMC : 452	□	= DMC : 932
◸	= DMC : 3362	Λ	= DMC : 223	○	= DMC : 502	↓	= DMC : Blanc
7	= DMC : 3727	▲	= DMC : 221	▼	= DMC : 935		

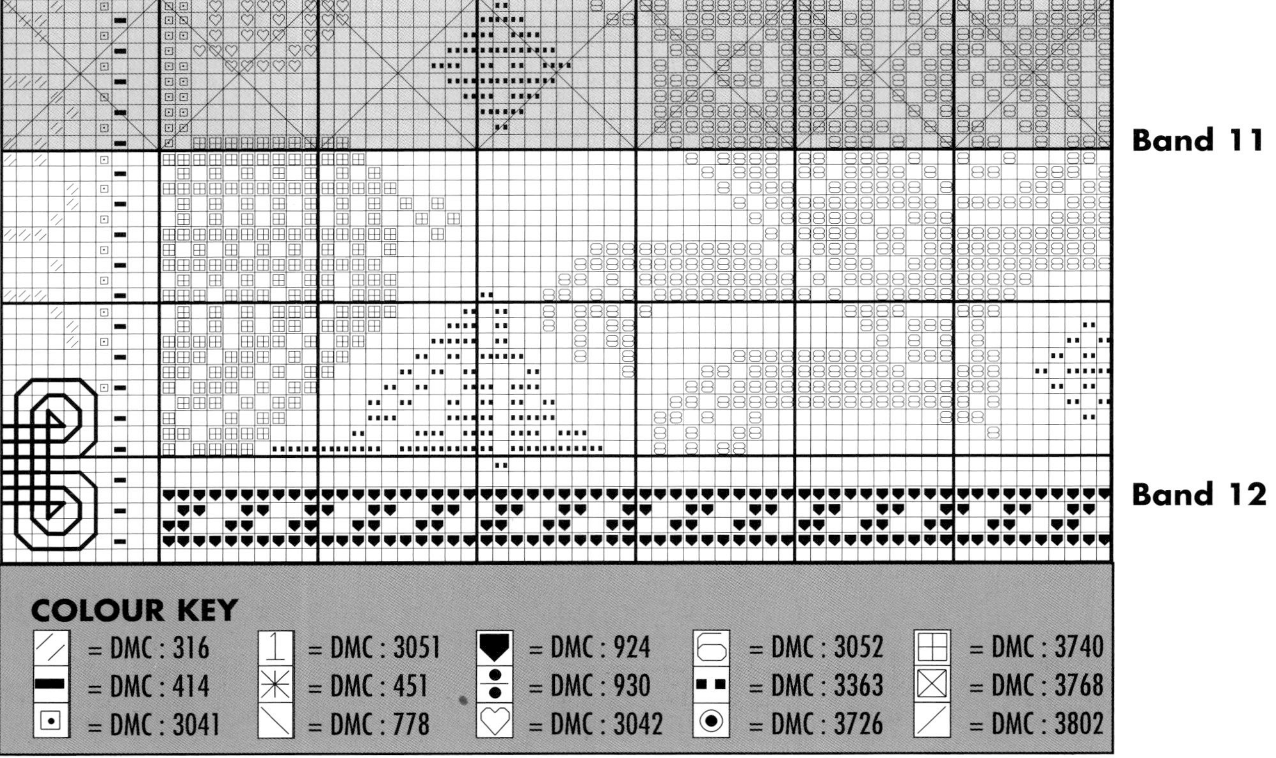

Band 11
Band 12
COLOUR KEY
= DMC : 316
= DMC : 414
= DMC : 3041
= DMC : 3051
= DMC : 451
= DMC : 778
= DMC : 924
= DMC : 930
= DMC : 3042
= DMC : 3052
= DMC : 3363
= DMC : 3726
= DMC : 3740
= DMC : 3768
= DMC : 3802

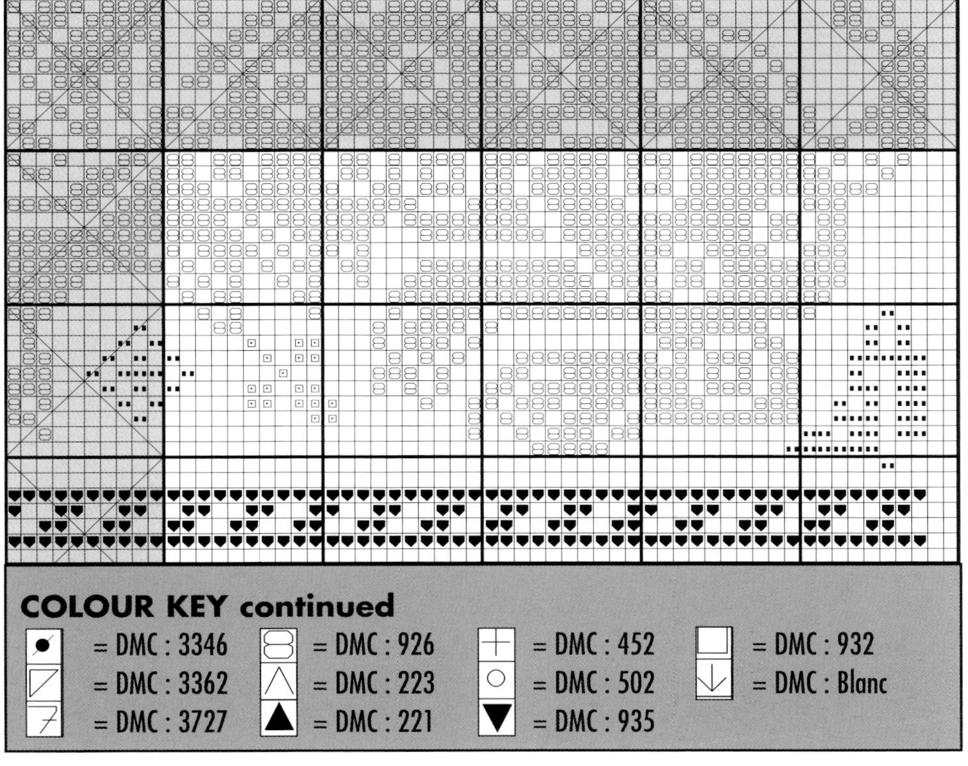

Fifth Section - right hand side of Double Band Sampler
Rest of band 11 and band 12

Shaded areas indicate overlaps from previous page
Refer to the colour photograph page 46 for additional detail

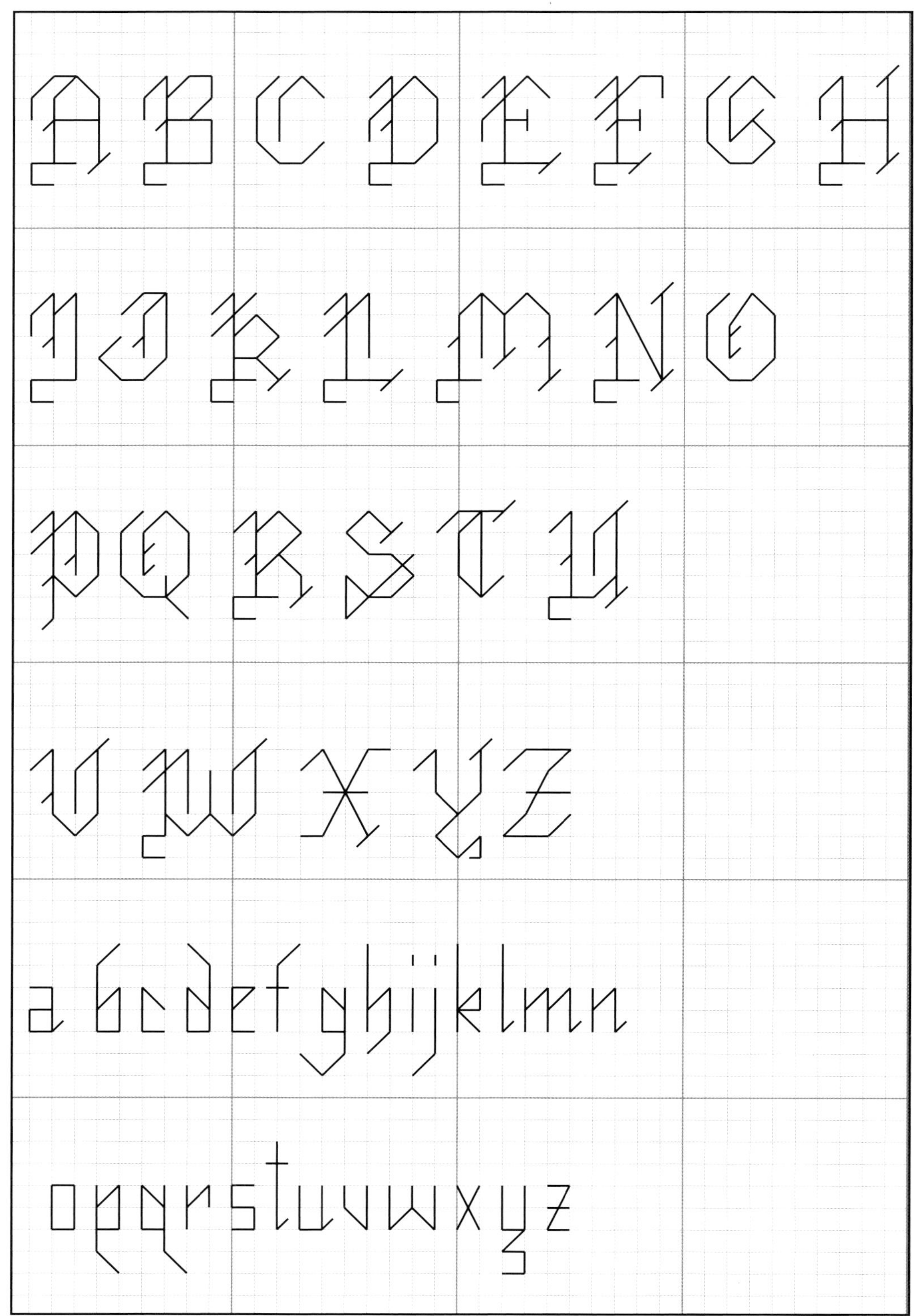

Alphabet and Numerals

Each square on this chart represents two threads of fabric

This is worked in Holbein or back stitch and is stitched using one thread of stranded cotton in the colour of your choice.